MELISSA ETHERIDGE:
Our Little Secret

MELISSA ETHERIDGE: OUR LITTLE SECRET

Joyce Luck

ECW PRESS

CANADIAN CATALOGUING IN PUBLICATION DATA

Luck, Joyce
Melissa Etheridge: our little secret

ISBN 1-55022-298-8

1. Etheridge, Melissa.   2. Rock musicians – United States – Biography.
3. Women rock musicians – United States – Biography   I. Title.

ML420.E88L82 1996   782.42166'092   C96-990101-1

Front-cover photo: Kevin Mazur / London Features International.
Back-cover photo: G. Dubose / London Features International.

Cover design, photo editing, and color section
by David Johnson and Glenna Vinokur
of Vinson Enterprises, Montreal.

Imaging by ECW Type & Art, Oakville, Ontario.
Printed by Kromar Printing, Winnipeg, Manitoba.

Distributed in Canada by General Distribution Services,
30 Lesmill Road, Don Mills, Ontario M3B 2T6.

Distributed in the United States by Login Publishers Consortium,
1436 West Randolph Street, Chicago, Illinois, U.S.A. 60607.

Published by ECW PRESS,
2120 Queen Street East, Suite 200,
Toronto, Ontario M4E 1E2.

www.ecw.ca / press

ACKNOWLEDGMENTS

For research help, I am indebted to the following people: in the United States, Taylor Banaszak, Kim Giardina, Deb Hanrahan, Elise Kantor, Tori Oster, Lou Roberts, Valerie and Marilyn Smith, and Dawn Soldan; in Canada, David Johnson; in Australia, Heidi MacKenzie; in the Netherlands, Florence Bouvier. Thanks also go to Lynn Needs for her photographic expertise, and to everyone who provided me with the wonderful stories and snapshots — I only wish I could have included half of what was given to me. Thanks also go to Mary Williams, the world's best editor, and to David and Glenna for the world's greatest discography. To my son, David: your curiosity is an inspiration. To Beth, who sweated over the manuscript when I thrust it under her nose at the worst of times: I love you. And, of course, to Melissa Etheridge and Julie Cypher. I am forever grateful to you all.

TABLE OF CONTENTS

One

OUT OF KANSAS: COMING ALIVE IN THE MIDWEST

If you head north out of Kansas City on Highway 7 and travel on for about forty-five minutes, you'll come upon Leavenworth, Kansas, sprawling peacefully across the Midwestern plain from the banks of the Missouri River. Here, on the north side of town near the famous federal penitentiary, Melissa Lou Etheridge was born on 29 May 1961 at 1:15 in the afternoon.

★ ★ ★

Flash forward: 12 November 1994. She's come home. It's a Saturday night in Leavenworth. The high-school auditorium air thickens with nervous energy; the place is jam-packed. Everybody is here, from a little neighbor kid to a couple in their fifties who live over on the next block. Even some of the high-school teachers dot the crowd. This looks like an audience for a school play. It isn't. The buzz of the crowd is getting louder and more urgent. People lean in closer, pressing towards the front of the hall. The space seems to swell.

Finally, a lone male figure strolls onto the stage to introduce the woman everyone has been waiting for. He welcomes the crowd. Everyone listens with mounting impatience as he adds, "Melissa is a hometown girl . . . her father was very active in our community . . . we are going to dedicate the ball field in her name (sorry, in *John's* name)" — the one in the "new park we're getting ready to build." The $20 each person has spent on his or her ticket will go towards that project, the man reminds the audience; then he points out that ushers in orange vests are still collecting money at the back of the auditorium.

Several women scream, drowning out whatever he has left to say. Melissa Etheridge and her band have taken the stage. The crowd leaps up with a roar as Etheridge and the band explode into "If I Wanted To"; then they segue into "No Souvenirs." Dressed in black pants, a T-shirt, and a loose-fitting rust-colored overshirt, sleeves rolled up and head thrown back, Melissa plays ferociously, thrusting the neck of her Ovation guitar up into the air, her strumming fingers a blur. The hall rocks as it has never rocked before.

★ ★ ★

In Leavenworth, military personnel and civilians, solid citizens and out-and-out rebels have found a way to coexist. Each June, a thousand officers and their families, stationed at Fort Leavenworth, move in and out of town. F. Scott Fitzgerald, author of *The Great Gatsby*, entered the army here at the age of twenty-one. Everyone knows about the pen: the forbidding federal prison was home to the likes of Al Capone. But that's not all Leavenworth is famous for: local lore has it that Pulman's Diner serves the best onion rings around.

The old-timers like to spin yarns of how the city — founded in 1854 — and the surrounding area became home to four prisons: the federal pen, the Kansas Penitentiary at Lansing, the Kansas Women's Prison at Lansing, and the U.S. Army Disciplinary Barracks at Fort Leavenworth. Sometime during the 1880s, the citizens of Leavenworth, "The First City of Kansas" (a sign on a downtown building still bears this proud designation today), were offered a choice: their city could be the site of a new federal penitentiary or the new University of Kansas, to be built under the recently passed Land Grant University Act. After much deliberation, the citizenry settled on the prison — because, as the old-timers claim, they reckoned it would attract a better class of people to the town.

It could only happen in Leavenworth. Here, a schoolgirl taking her seat in the classroom can easily find herself with a farmer's daughter on one side and a prison guard's son on the other. Just in front of her could be a child whose uncle works at the Hallmark candle factory, and directly behind her might sit an immigrant from Germany. A town full of ironies, Leavenworth is largely conservative due to its military influence; yet, because of Fort Leavenworth's officer training school, the very thing that makes the town conservative also brings it a certain cultural energy and diversity. This is due to the fact that many of the thousand officers stationed here on a temporary basis are funneled in from the Allied forces: the flavors of the Philippines, the Central and South American countries, and England add spice to the Midwestern ambience.

Boasting about forty thousand inhabitants, Leavenworth is a small town in a national context; but, on a local scale, it is a good-sized city — the population of Kansas as a whole is only about 2.5 million. Rayna Wagley, a native, mentions the claustrophobia she felt growing up in the town. She remarks that the penitentiary lent a certain negativity, or bad karma, to the atmosphere, and that the town's teenagers were aimless and bored. Scores of kids used drugs back when Rayna was growing up, and so she admires Melissa Etheridge for having emerged from that environment without falling into the enticing trap of drugs and alcohol.

Celebrities often ridicule their home towns, and Leavenworth could seem a legitimate target to many. Lack of sophistication or worldliness is always a good source for easy jokes. The opening of the Leavenworth outlet of Pier 1 Imports in the late seventies was a major event in town. When Melissa was a child, there was only one local AM radio station; no FM stations existed until she was a teenager. But, points out Kim Clair, a childhood friend of Etheridge's, Melissa "has never said anything bad about this town."

In fact, in 1989, Melissa returned to Leavenworth to celebrate her ten-year high-school reunion (where she was voted the alumna with "Most Appearances on the David Letterman Show"), and returned again in November of 1994 to visit family and perform a benefit at her old high school for the projected South Leavenworth Park (which has yet to materialize). While there, she also donated a generous sum in her father's name to refurbish the Performing Arts Center, and instituted a performing-arts scholarship for high-school students. In a *Rolling Stone* interview published shortly after that second visit home, Melissa remarked: "I'm glad I grew up in a small town. . . . I grew up with huge dreams, and yet I had this sort of small-town sensibility. I had what I call values. But they're certainly not what I mean by morality. You learn to treat people good. There was a real work ethic. And I can't help but be very open and very straightforward. People think rock & rollers are supposed to have this attitude, and I've never had that" ("Melissa Etheridge: In through the Out Door").

★   ★   ★

Life, for Melissa Etheridge, began on north-side Potta-

watomie Street in a section of Leavenworth inhabited
by young families. The neighborhood swarmed with
children. (The Etheridges later moved to nearby Miami
Street.) Kim Clair remembers climbing with Missy (as
everybody called Melissa back then) on the jungle gym in
Kim's backyard, and recalls how tomboyish they were,
playing cowboys and sloshing through mud puddles.
Missy was well liked. She hosted sleepovers, and, a little
later on, as a junior-high student, threw make-out parties
in her basement. Oblivious to the goings-on below, the
senior Etheridges sat quietly upstairs. Kim says that in
the sixth grade Missy's boyfriend was Mike Strange — like
Missy, a budding musician. The pair dated on and off all
through their junior-high years, and both played guitar for
the high-school chorale.

Melissa and Mike Strange, from the 1977
Leavenworth High School Yearbook
COURTESY LEAVENWORTH HIGH SCHOOL

Melissa's early family life was pretty much like that of any other Midwestern kid. Her favorite toys were her Rock 'Em Sock 'Em Robots; she got into big trouble once for crawling down the storm drain outside her house. John Etheridge, her father, taught history, psychology, and government at Leavenworth High School. He also coached basketball. Elizabeth, her mother, was a computer specialist for the army. Melissa also has a sister, Jenny, who is four years older. Kim Clair comments that she never actually saw the Etheridges interact much as a family. "I remember [Melissa's] mom was kind of quiet."

A woman with few friends, Elizabeth Etheridge appears always to have been a practical-minded, introverted kind of person, preferring to spend time alone reading. At first, she did not embrace her daughter's musical career as

John Etheridge, from the 1977 Leavenworth High School Yearbook

COURTESY
LEAVENWORTH
HIGH SCHOOL

enthusiastically as her husband did. In fact, it wasn't until Melissa reached the age of twenty-five that mother and daughter really began communicating with each other. But Melissa has admitted that she thinks miscommunication is "a common mother-daughter thing. [My mother] went through some changes, and we are now the best of friends, just wonderfully communicative" ("Melissa Etheridge," *Us*). Now the two talk on the phone regularly. Elizabeth Etheridge even flew into Leavenworth from her current home in northwestern Arkansas to attend the 1994 benefit concert. Her mother is "very, very intelligent," Melissa says, and has even become "a little activist herself" ("Melissa Etheridge: LN's Exclusive Interview").

At Leavenworth High — home of Pioneer Pete, a coonskin-cap-wearing mascot — John Etheridge is fondly remembered as a teacher and as coach of the Leavenworth Pioneers. Virtually anyone will tell you how good he was at his job. Melissa has told her concert audiences that she would hear stories about her father from kids who'd had him as a teacher. He was so obviously proud of his rockstar daughter that his students eventually devised a way to turn that paternal pride to their own advantage: they would casually ask on the day a test was scheduled, "So, Mr. Etheridge, what's Melissa up to these days?" — at which point their teacher would launch into a thirty-minute monologue on the subject. Voila! No time for a test.

The son of a migrant farmer raised in southern Missouri during World War II, John Etheridge seems also to have been a troubled man at times. His childhood was marred by poverty, Melissa has revealed to *Rolling Stone*, and by becoming a schoolteacher he took one giant step away from the milieu of despair that might have laid permanent claim to him. Both John and Elizabeth Etheridge had alcoholic fathers. Common to children of alcoholics is the tendency to shut down emotionally —

anger is a particularly unacceptable emotion to display. Melissa also divulges this about her parents: "all they wanted was to forget their past. So I grew up in a house where everything was just fine. I wasn't abused. If I needed something, I had it. But there was no feeling. There was no joy, there was no sadness or pain. And then if there was pain, it was just a nod."

Melissa coped with this emotional vacuum by retreating to the basement recreation room to write songs. Music became her emotional release, and she also discovered that it was an effective tool to elicit a response from people. "It was OK to make people cry, but it wasn't OK to cry, you know?" she explained to *Rolling Stone*. To *Lesbian News*, Melissa remarked: "So as a child I was just filled with all this stuff — and where was I going to put it? Some children get angry and they do drugs and rebel. I went in the basement and wrote songs. I cultivated this anger and this fear and this sadness and longing into music."

After John Etheridge retired, he and Elizabeth moved to Arkansas; shortly after they were settled, John developed liver cancer. He died on 8 August 1991. In a 1994 *Advocate* interview that sparked some controversy, Melissa speculated about the root cause of her father's affliction: "I believe his illness was brought on by his difficult childhood. He kept his anger about his alcoholic parents inside himself. His anger turned to cancer. The body can only hold that stress in for so long before it becomes something else" ("Melissa: Rock's Great Dyke Hope"). Indignant readers accused Melissa of blaming a sick person for his own condition, and their accusations echoed those commonly leveled against people who attack the victims of AIDS for bringing the disease upon themselves. In a subsequent *Advocate* interview, Melissa took care to make it clear that she had been expressing a personal conviction, not making a sweeping statement about the nature of illness: "It is *my* belief, that's all. Julie [her life partner] still doesn't believe that I have ever gotten really angry around her, because it seems like nothing to her. But to me [getting angry is] scary, walls-falling-down horrible" ("Person of the Year").

Despite his problems, John Etheridge was a good and decent man who clung to hometown values. Melissa remembers that when she first performed publicly her father reminded her: "You should always thank your audience." The philosophy and the values that John Etheridge instilled in her have served Melissa well, both professionally and personally. Part of her staying power as a musician, she contends, is due to the fact that, unlike many rock stars, she has not taken on a nasty or condescending attitude. "My dad taught me differently," she says simply. "I could see him treat other people in a kind way, and when I tried it, it worked" ("Person of the Year").

Even while still in diapers, Melissa Etheridge loved music and dancing. When John or Elizabeth would spin a disk on the family's portable Philco 45, Melissa came alive. She would dance and clap in sheer delight to the strains of her parents' favorites: Simon and Garfunkel, Johnny Mathis, Neil Diamond, Della Reese, Aretha Franklin, and the Mamas and the Papas. At a tender age, she formed her first band: while Melissa vigorously strummed a tennis racket, several of her neighborhood pals accompanied her on pots and pans. At the age of eight, her father presented her with her first guitar — a Stella by Harmony. He had recognized her interest and talent. The Stella was eventually replaced by an Alvarez six-string. Before long, a pint-sized Melissa Etheridge was taking guitar lessons from Don Raymond, a jazz guitarist and owner, at the time, of the Toon Shop, Leavenworth's only music store. "He was real strict about timing," Melissa recalls. "He tapped his foot really loud on an old wooden board. He's the reason I have really good rhythm" (qtd. in Carswell).

At the age of ten, Melissa composed her first song, called "Don't Let It Fly Away, It's Love." She laughed as she admitted to *Rolling Stone*, "I rhymed everything: *love, above*; *bus* with *Gus*." The song had only two or three chords, and, as its composer remarked, "I was singing 'la la la we all need to love each other la la la' " (qtd. in Anderson). "It was an ecology, love-each-other song, because that was all I knew," she added. "Hey, it was the early 70s, and I just heard my first Joan Baez song" (qtd. in Baumgardner).

Another song that Etheridge wrote as a child is "The Old Man." To the best recollection of Dawn Soldan — who once heard Melissa perform it at the Que Sera Sera club in Long Beach — it's about an old man who lives in a shack on the edge of town. He is befriended by a young child, but the child's mother warns her to keep away from him. One day, the mother searches for her wayward daughter and finds her near the shack. The little girl tries to explain to her mother about the old man, but when she looks back, she discovers he is gone.

Today when she reflects on these early songs, Etheridge concedes that she was mimicking the protest songs of the era. Music seemed magical to her then because it had the inherent power to make social statements and render strong emotions clear. It also allowed Melissa to feel special among her friends — they would come over to her house and coax her to play for them. Melissa says, "they loved [my songs]. And they would listen. And I would receive something back from it. And from this grew the desire to [write music] more and to work on it and make it grow. It was a talent" ("Melissa Etheridge: LN's Exclusive Interview").

When she was eleven years old, Etheridge entered a talent contest held at the Leavenworth Plaza Tower. It was her first public appearance. Missy sang "Lonely as a Child," an original, heart-wrenching song about war in a foreign country; in it, a child's mother is killed. The song packed an emotional wallop — it was the era of the Vietnam War — and Melissa's musical precocity was irresistible. According to a number of sources, she won the contest. But in a 1989 Dutch television interview, Melissa contradicted this version of events. Not only, she maintained, did she not perform alone (two of her friends sang with her), but she also ranked only about tenth overall. Still, her first experience of performing publicly was a significant one. It has remained etched in Etheridge's memory, perhaps because, as a result of that contest, Melissa and a group of other musicians put together a show that toured local schools, nursing homes, and prisons.

By the time she was twelve, Etheridge was a part-time musician in a local country-and-western band called the Wranglers. Her first gig was at Bud and Fay's Bar in Leavenworth. Country was the first style of music that Etheridge ever performed consistently — a predictable and realistic choice for a girl growing up in the heart of the Midwestern farming belt. She covered all the old chestnuts: " 'Stand By Your Man,' 'The End of the World' . . . stuff like that" (qtd. in Everett). Most probably, she learned song structure from doing those country standards: "verse-chorus-bridge-chorus-out" (qtd. in Zollo).

Other early music influences included the Archies — the Saturday-morning-cartoon band based on that timeless gang of comic-book high-school buddies and sweethearts. Melissa confides that Reggie was her favorite: "He was definitely the coolest. I wanted to be Reggie. He was dark, he was bad. Someday I would like to do a cover of 'Sugar, Sugar' — it's a great song" (qtd. in Zollo). She was serious. She actually did cover this song while performing at Vermie's, a women's bar in Pasadena, California, but only after being coerced by a persistent member of the audience. In a 1996 Rockline interview, Etheridge joked that one day she'd like to slip the song into the middle of one of her concerts, just when everyone is getting down and dirty. Another popular kid-oriented group of the time that the young Etheridge did *not* like or respect was the Partridge Family: "They faked their music and that bugged the hell out of me" (qtd. in Carswell). Like so many kids of her age, she tuned in faithfully to *American Bandstand* and *Soul Train*.

Melissa's country-and-western group was regularly hired for gigs such as Parents without Partners dances, and appeared at the Knights of Columbus Hall, the Veterans of Foreign Wars Hall, and the National Guard Armory. In bars, mostly neighborhood country dives, Melissa would play with the band for the first hour and then leave with her father, who wanted to ensure that she got to bed at a decent hour. But these paternal measures were not enough to shield her from the rough-and-tumble code of such drinking establishments. Melissa recalls crouching behind a Hammond organ to avoid getting nailed by flying bottles during one bar brawl.

Guitar in hand, Melissa also tagged along with John Etheridge when he attended teachers' conventions organized by the National Education Association. And before too long, Missy Etheridge was a familiar face in Leavenworth, adding bowling alleys and supermarket openings to her list of venues. She even played at the pen. "Prisons have the most enthusiastic audiences," she observed. There she could find the ultimate captive audience: "2,000 people who all want to be entertained" (qtd. in Carswell).

Yet as a child Melissa could not, according to some, even carry a tune. There are those who say that she sang in a church choir, but was made to stand at the outer reaches

Sophomore Yearbook photo (1977)

Junior Yearbook photo (1978)

Senior Yearbook photo (1979)

ALL PHOTOS COURTESY
LEAVENWORTH HIGH SCHOOL

when the choristers were assigned their places. This was done at the request of the reverend, who found her voice too hoarse and penetrating. Elizabeth Etheridge herself has said that "Early on, [Melissa] didn't have a great voice. . . . I think some people are born with a singing voice, but I don't think she was. She just realized that was part of what she wanted to do, and she taught herself" (qtd. in Dunn "Melissa Etheridge"). John and Elizabeth enrolled their musically precocious child in the voice-training sessions being offered by a Leavenworth classical vocalist, but after a mere two weeks Melissa was dismissed by her trainer on the grounds that nothing could be done for her. The problem, of course, may simply have been that Melissa wasn't interested in opera — she wanted to belt out rock and roll.

By the time she entered high school, Etheridge was performing in a band called Roadshow. "She's been in a band for as long as I've known her," says David Ramos, a friend from those high-school years. Melissa had been a bit of a jock in junior high, becoming a member of the girl's basketball team; she had also played bass clarinet in the junior-high band. Such pursuits, however, were abandoned as the high-school era dawned. By that time, Melissa could also play drums, saxophone, and keyboards, and there was no holding her back. As well, she had gone from playing a six-string to a twelve-string acoustic guitar because she loved the bigger sound. The first of these was a Guild twelve-string, but it was just too large for the petite Etheridge; so she switched again at age fourteen to a Pacemaker, made by Ovation, and has had an Ovation ever since (Resnicoff). Etheridge's current instrument of choice is a custom-made Adamas with a cutaway.

The "music and drama weirdos" formed Melissa's crowd in high school. "We were very creative and very strange," she told her *Rolling Stone* interviewer. During her sophomore year, she played the role of Mrs. Blair in the drama club's production of *Inherit the Wind*, a play about the famous 1925 Scopes trial, which hinged on a Tennessee law forbidding the teaching of evolution in state-supported schools. There were over sixty extras in the production, many of them the younger brothers and sisters of primary cast members. While a high-school student, Etheridge also appeared in *Oklahoma* (as Aunt Eller) and the *Wizard of Oz* (as Dorothy). In her junior year, Melissa was awarded the school's best-actress prize. She was also active in the French club; a fellow student recalls that Melissa taught club members to sing American pop songs in French. Others remember Etheridge performing Bee Gees and Commodores tunes at the prom. Somehow, she was able to sandwich in a part-time job as a packer at Kentucky Fried Chicken. Despite all this feverish activity, she still managed to be a good student: during her senior year, she was a member of the National Honor Society.

Lester Dalton was director of Leavenworth High's music groups while Melissa was in her junior and senior years. Though there was a general choir open to all students, there was also a select choir comprised of those with superior voices. The best of the best, however, were invited into the chorale: by this time, Melissa had developed her singing talent enough to be included in this exclusive ensemble. "Her intensity was apparent, even when she was a young teenager," Dalton enthused on a VH-1 special covering Etheridge's 1994 hometown concert. "The talent was absolutely magnificent. She could do anything."

Power and Life — as the chorale called itself — toured the area under Dalton's stewardship, singing for local clubs and schools. Some people didn't like Power and Life's selections, however; many of the songs were religious, and the group seemed strongly attracted to summer- camp fare,

Melissa as Aunt Eller in a school production
of Oklahoma, *from the 1979 Yearbook*
PHOTOS COURTESY LEAVENWORTH HIGH SCHOOL

such as "Kum Ba Yah." But in Leavenworth during the 1970s, such musical preferences would hardly have been objectionable to the mainstream. One math teacher, for example, used to bring her guitar to school and perform religious songs for her students.

The Youth of the Chapel (YOC), which, among other things, wrote and performed its own musicals, also benefited from the burgeoning musical talents of Melissa Etheridge. A church group sponsored by Protestant chaplain services, YOC was headquartered at Fort Leavenworth. Though devout, the group was fairly open-minded, non-denominational, and ecumenical in orientation. "Everyone was welcome," says David Ramos, who, along with his twin brother, Richard, and Melissa, was an active YOC member. In 1977, YOC staged a production of *Godspell*. Melissa played lead guitar, David played rhythm guitar, and Richard did the bass work. David insists that Melissa "was the energy behind it. She took some pretty amateur musicians and made us sound good." Their efforts were so well received that an extra night was added to the performance schedule. Afterwards, Melissa sold David her purple Fender Telecaster for $250, writing in his high-school yearbook later that year: "I hope you enjoy my guitar! You can paint it a different color if you want. I sure am gonna miss it so take care of it!! And when I become a great star you can play guitar on my albums OK? It's a deal! Take care! Love Ya Lots!! Missy E.!!"

Etheridge never made a secret of her aspirations. She had wanted stardom, pure and simple, for as long as she could remember. Her high-school peers didn't doubt her for a second: "Missy E." was a young woman of prodigious talent, unquenchable energy — and big ideas. In 1978, she contributed all the music and a good portion of the lyrics to another YOC musical, this one conceived and created by the group itself. It was called *82nd Street Park*.

Then, in her senior year, Melissa wrote yet another musical, basing it on two books of the Bible and calling it *Nazera*. Richard Ramos describes another instance of Melissa's propensity to think big. Being from a military family, and being members of the JROTC, David and Richard were both pilots as well as amateur musicians. In April of 1979, the YOC went on a retreat. Closing ceremonies were planned, and Melissa, slated to bring the proceedings to an end, came up with the following idea. She would ask the audience this question: "If you thought about what you wanted most from God, what would it be?" As she did this, she would raise her hand and stretch it towards the sky. Richard was to take this as his cue to fly over the assembled and shower them with marshmallows inscribed with the words "God Loves You." "I was running a little late," he now laughs. "I flew over and dumped them . . . I don't know if I even hit."

It's not easy to determine how religious a person Etheridge actually was at this age. She certainly believed in some kind of higher power, and the religious groups to which she belonged had provided her with a good outlet for her musical talents. Yet she has denied ever being drawn to organized religion, saying that, though she was raised a Methodist (which she calls "religion lite"), she "knew it was all just a big story" (qtd. in Carswell). And, although she played in so many Leavenworth churches, she now explains that she "was never of the mind that I believed what was going on. I thought it was very curious, the organized religion, but I felt that there was a greater spirituality than these rules and this judgment that these people were laying down. And I still have a real hard time with organized religion. I think that it's the root of a lot of our problems" (qtd. in Phoenix).

As she was developing this critical distance from the structured form of religious expression she had been brought up to participate in, Melissa was undergoing yet another spiritual/emotional change. Sometime during these high-school years, Etheridge became aware of her growing sexual attraction to other girls, even though she was still drawn (if only by convention) to guys. The transformation was mainly a private one. In fact, Kim Clair remarks that when Melissa came out in 1993, many of those who had known her in Leavenworth were stunned by the revelation.

But at this point in her young life Melissa Etheridge was still entranced by music above all else. By now, she had been introduced to rock-and-roll acts such as Led Zeppelin, Steppenwolf, Humble Pie, Jethro Tull, Bob Seger, and Bruce Springsteen. Her mentor in this musical expansion was big sister Jenny, who had become a typical rebellious teenager and was constantly in trouble at home. Songs like Springsteen's "Jungleland" captivated Melissa; she'd disappear into her room armed with eight-track tapes and headphones and get lost for hours, transported (as she told *Rolling Stone*) to an alternate reality by the sheer emotion of the music. Melissa even remembers one summer listening to the Beatles' *Sgt. Pepper* album every single day (see Zollo).

Music was, for Melissa, a source of adventure, of discovery, while sexuality was no doubt a source of confusion: adolescence is traumatic and bewildering enough without the question of homosexuality being added to the mix. It seems inevitable, though, that Etheridge's preoccupations would merge and enhance one another on some level. Writing songs actually became a way of examining her attraction to girls. In fact, she admits, "I used to sing Springsteen songs at the top of my lungs when I was a kid because he was singing about a girl and I could relate" (qtd. in Kennedy). At seventeen, she realized she had fallen in love with her best friend. On Melissa's birthday, they shared a kiss, and in that moment she was forced to confront the source of her indifference towards conventional romantic love and guys: Why did those essentials of dawning heterosexuality that had fired so many of her peers feel like a "take-it-or-leave-it" proposition to her? Melissa realized that boys bored her emotionally, that she had never experienced "that heart-pounding thing" when she was with them (qtd. in Kennedy).

An interviewer pursued the topic of young romance when speaking to Melissa in 1995. "A large part of . . . high school life is the boys chasing the girls and, if they get lucky, 'running the bases,' " he remarked, and then asked Etheridge if she'd been a part of all that. "I would say I ran the bases out of curiosity," she responded. "But [I was] very, totally unpassionate about it. No involvement at all . . . just enough to go, 'OK, that's what this is' " ("Melissa Etheridge," *Us*).

Before the kiss, before the revelation, however, there must have been moments of intuition, periods of unexpressed internal struggle; the scribbling about powerful and baffling feelings in gender-neutral songs was just a surface manifestation. David Ramos recalls that Missy and her best friend would occasionally call him to come and pick them up in his car. They'd drive around for awhile, and then park and talk for hours on end. "I think she may have been probing at that point," David admits, although he is quick to concur that today he has the benefit of hindsight; he doesn't recall even considering at that time the possibility that Melissa was a lesbian. David knows that he wouldn't have been Melissa's first choice of confidante. He also recognizes that he — and most of Leavenworth — would not have been able to understand or accept her lesbianism. "*Everybody* [was] conservative and clean-cut," Richard Ramos interjects.

Melissa and her best friend, who was also active in YOC,

did attempt to talk to an adult member of that group about the physical turn their relationship had taken. "The advice they received was, 'Just stop!'" They had hit the brick wall of small-town conservatism before they'd even begun their journey. "There was really no one else to talk to," Melissa explains. "You feel crazy, and then the rumors start because you spend so much time together" (qtd. in Carswell). About a year after David graduated from high school, the rumor reached him that Etheridge was gay. His immediate reaction was denial: "Not Missy!" he recalls thinking. But even back then, he ultimately chose to overlook the question of his friend's sexuality because "she was such a quality human being."

"Missy is a lezzie," some self-appointed sexual-conduct monitor scrawled across a Leavenworth High bathroom wall for all the world to see. "I didn't really care because I knew I was leaving," Melissa told *Rolling Stone*. "I was out of there."

Two

COLLEGE DAYS

Boston, Massachusetts. Home of the Red Sox and Fenway Park. Home of the Boston Celtics and the Bruins. Home of the 2.5-mile Freedom Trail, which traces 350 years of American history. Home of the U.S. Navy's oldest surviving ship, the *U.S.S. Constitution* (better known as "Old Ironsides"), built in 1797. Home of the bar Cheers, of television sitcom fame. And home of award-winning Samuel Adams beer, probably America's best brew — at least until the microbrewery craze took hold.

This is a city steeped in American history. An early Puritan colony, Boston became a major shipping center shortly after it was founded. When Mother Britain imposed commercial restrictions that affected the colony's overseas trade, the colonists rebelled. Enraged Bostonians clashed with British soldiers, and a number of the colonists were shot and killed. Dressed as Native Americans, another band of furious colonists dumped British tea into Boston Harbor to protest the tea tax and British import restrictions. Two years after the Boston Massacre and the Boston Tea Party, Paul Revere rode out from Boston at midnight to warn Minutemen in the surrounding country-side that the British redcoats were coming. The Lexington Green skirmish and the battle at Concord Bridge occurred the following day, and constituted the first official instances of bloodshed in the American Revolutionary War. Later, during the Civil War era, the city came out strongly against slavery. Boston was home to many important abolitionists, among them literary figures Ralph Waldo Emerson and James Russell Lowell. In fact, so many early literary icons have hailed from Boston that the city has been called the "Athens of America" — some of the most celebrated are Hawthorne, Thoreau, Howells, and Fuller.

Boston is also the home of Berklee College of Music, and this alone is what mattered to eighteen-year-old Melissa Etheridge, newly released from Leavenworth High and primed to launch her musical career. She arrived on a sweltering August day in 1979, and was unimpressed by her new surroundings. She would later admit that she never really learned to like the place while living there. Today, though, she remembers Boston fondly because it gave her an opportunity to meet an entire community of gay women.

John and Elizabeth Etheridge were all for their youngest daughter attending college, and Melissa was ready to comply, as long as she could go to a school where she could pursue her first love: guitar. This stipulation nixed such institutions as New York's Juilliard School of Music, which was more distinguished as a school for voice. Her parents, Melissa says, "knew that music made me happy and that I was good at it. I knew how to read music pretty well, and at Berklee you could major in guitar." Etheridge gained acceptance into the Berklee program without difficulty, and was thoroughly unintimidated by the school's reputation as a "hothouse for aspiring musicians" (qtd. in Everett 47).

The city of Boston itself, on the other hand, was no doubt a bit of a shock to the teenager fresh from the Midwestern plains. Asked to describe the transition from Leavenworth to Boston, she responded: "Huge change [laughs]. You know, I had travelled around, it wasn't like I hadn't been to other cities. I had relatives in Los Angeles and Atlanta and some big cities and I'd seen them. I wasn't afraid of Boston. I do remember the first night I spent there, there was a mouse in my room. And I couldn't sleep because of all the sirens going off. But it only takes a few weeks to get used to that" ("Kansas Girl"). Etheridge did not have to deal with loneliness, though. Her best friend and lover (whose name is withheld here out of respect for her privacy) joined her in Boston shortly after her arrival.

The two stayed until April of 1981. Melissa's college career spanned three semesters, although she completed only two; Berklee records simply indicate that she was there for a year. Despite the brevity of her tenure, however, Etheridge did not leave college empty-handed: Berklee granted her a professional music diploma with a major in guitar and voice on 1 May 1980. According to a representative of the college, diplomas are conferred even if a student doesn't complete the bachelor's degree, which requires both the music diploma and completion of the more standard baccalaureate degree courses, such as English. But the music diploma was not Etheridge's only reward — she also gained admission to a select group of female Berklee graduates who have gone on to achieve stardom, including Aimee Mann (who was awarded her degree the same year as Etheridge, and who had bright green hair at the time), Lisa Loeb, Paula Cole, and Melissa Ferrick.

Lauren Passarelli and Cindy Brown — both of whom attended Berklee with Melissa and numbered among her closest college friends — recall that Melissa maintained a dorm room on the campus for the sake of convenience.

Melissa's apartment at 53 Hereford Street in Boston
KIM GIARDINA

She also rented an apartment on Newberry Street with her lover, and they later moved to a one-bedroom apartment with a loft bed that was suspended from the ceiling. This second apartment, at 53 Hereford Street, cost the couple around $80 or $90 a month to rent. Melissa's lover helped out a little by taking babysitting jobs, but it was Melissa who covered most of the expenses. One of the jobs she undertook was security guard at Deaconess Hospital; for this she had to wear a uniform, which, Lauren laughs, could only be described as "dorky."

Etheridge even raised some cash busking on city sidewalks and possibly even in the subway stations. Busking is "good experience, very humbling," she later told an Australian television interviewer. Many Etheridge fans have long insisted that the song "Watching You," which was included on Etheridge's first album, was a product of her experience as a busker. The story goes that Melissa would regularly watch a woman toiling in a nearby office building from her subway-stop vantage point, and found herself imagining what it would be like to be caught in the woman's daily routine. Etheridge finally set the record straight on VH-1's *Storytellers* in November of 1996. After leaving Boston, she wrote "Watching You" while reminiscing about a crush she once had on a woman there. Strolling down Newberry Street in the summer heat to the sound of music blaring from wide-open windows, she would gaze up at one particular apartment, the home of a woman who never even knew Melissa existed. She would be filled with hunger and loneliness.

By far her most lucrative gig, however, was performing at Ken's by George on Boylston Street, a subterranean bar-restaurant right across from posh Copley Square. Working five nights a week at $50 per night, Melissa took on the role of lounge singer, playing piano and singing cover songs, many of which were show tunes. The clientele was mainly the businessmen who were staying at nearby hotels. They tended to be big tippers. Consequently, Lauren and Cindy say, Melissa always had money while the rest of them — penniless college students — just scraped by and prayed for a gig. Performing a few years later for a lesbian crowd at the Que Sera Sera in southern California, Melissa would joke about her lounge-lizard act back in Boston. Dawn Soldan, who caught many of those Que Sera Sera shows, says that Melissa used to make fun of her Boston self — that hard-working crooner who'd don a dress and shave her legs and armpits smooth. Lauren adds more detail to the portrait: Melissa, she remarks, was quite a bit heavier in Boston (as were Lauren and Cindy, due to their passion for Emack and Bolio's ice cream), and she had short, reddish-brown hair, which she wore in a tight perm.

Melissa was generous with her earnings. In fact, "she was *extremely* generous," Lauren says. She often treated Lauren and Cindy to dinner. The two would be sitting in their dorm room when they would hear Melissa and her lover shouting "We've got pizza! Lauren and Cindy, let us in!" Melissa would also surprise them with gifts. Cindy remembers that Melissa gave her and Lauren a pair of stuffed monkeys with their arms clasped tightly around each other and a copy of one of Melissa's favorite childhood books, William Steig's CDB. The book consists of a series of letters that make word sounds, and these correspond to pictures; for example, the title reads "C-D-B" (or "See the bee"), and on the cover is a picture of a little boy pointing to a flower over which a bee is hovering. When Melissa and her lover returned to Kansas in April of 1981, Melissa gave many of the couple's household items to Lauren and Cindy — she knew they could use them.

Lauren and Cindy actually met Melissa and her partner in May of 1980 through a friend named Julie, another Berklee student. The four of them — Lauren and Cindy and Melissa and her girlfriend — eventually became quite close because their situations were similar. Cindy and Lauren were a gay couple who felt they had to remain in the closet because they were active in Christian circles. Melissa, also, "was really into being Christian at that time," according to Cindy. This set of friendships was formally initiated when Melissa invited Cindy and Lauren home to talk and to listen to her play some of her music (she actually performed all of *Nazera*, her YOC musical, for them in one sitting). But Melissa had already known the potential for a lasting relationship was there. On the very first day she met Lauren and Cindy she had been feeling unusually discouraged. She had run into the pair sitting outside Emack and Bolio's eating ice cream, Lauren says, and confided that she "had been crying and praying to the Lord all day" because she just wasn't sure she belonged in Boston. There were a number of reasons for this.

At Berklee, Melissa was very much "a fish out of water," Lauren says. It was then primarily a jazz school, and pop rock wasn't (and still isn't) truly respected. Lauren, currently a professor at Berklee, explains that rock and roll is still young as an art form and still does not have an established "history of real musicianship." Melissa has said many times that the reason she decided to leave Berklee was that she wanted to go to Los Angeles to get on with her music career; Berklee, she felt, tended to dictate to its students how they should write songs, and she already knew how to do that.

Lauren feels Melissa didn't give Berklee enough of a chance. Certainly the basic courses in music theory were pretty rudimentary — chord progressions, and so on — but Melissa wasn't around long enough to get into the upper-level courses. At this stage, students are able to work with professors who are interested in them as individual musicians — "they get into the good stuff." Berklee has gotten much better in this regard, Lauren concludes. The school now spends more time teaching songwriting as a craft. Melissa today concedes that had she stayed at Berklee longer, she might have become a more versatile guitarist: "Now that I'm older and I've done music, I've found that there's a real place for [music theory], and that it's a way to communicate. I kind of wish today that I'd stayed and learned more technical aspects of guitar playing. I mean, I'm *not* a lead guitar player, and I regret that I didn't learn a lot of different chord forms" (qtd. in Resnicoff).

Was Melissa a good student during the brief period she spent at Berklee? Lauren doesn't know. She was a year ahead of Melissa, and wasn't in any classes with her. But, Lauren recollects with a smile, her own grades suffered when she was hanging out with Melissa and her lover because sometimes they'd all be up talking until two or three in the morning.

Berklee alumnus Peter Johnson recalls that Melissa was in a couple of his classes, including Listening Analysis (commonly known as "listening paralysis"). He describes seeing his old classmate perform in Ames, Iowa, in the late 1980s. The venue was small, and there were some empty seats in the front, so he and a companion positioned themselves there. After striking up a conversation with a member of the road crew, Peter mentioned that he was once in several of Melissa's classes in school. The next thing he knew, the roadie disappeared behind the scenes and reemerged with two all-access passes. So, Peter says, they joined the "grip and grin" after the show. He finally had the opportunity to talk with Melissa, and after awhile she looked at him and said, point-blank, "I don't remember you from high school." When Peter explained that it was *Berklee* he'd been talking about, they shared a laugh.

This incident suggests that in Melissa's mind, "school" is Leavenworth High, not Berklee College of Music. And maybe that's why she hasn't agreed to conduct guitar clinics at Berklee, despite having been invited to do so; neither has she responded to the college's requests for permission to run her photo on the cover of *Berklee Today*. Lauren suspects that Melissa is simply not comfortable drawing attention to herself as a Berklee graduate because she wasn't there all that long, and never really fit in when she was.

Melissa's feelings about Berklee might also have been influenced by the fact that she was not the "star" in Boston that she had been in Leavenworth. Berklee was packed with talented musicians, and at that time Etheridge was no more talented than anybody else. "In our eyes, we were *all* future rock stars," Lauren says. "But [becoming a star is] like hitting the lottery — very few people do." When Melissa actually did end up "hitting the lottery," Lauren and Cindy were both bowled over, and, they admit with obvious good humor, they were also very, very jealous. They found out about Melissa's success entirely by accident. Cindy happened to be in Harvard Square and wandered into a record store. Her eyes fell upon a blaring red album cover, and with a shock she registered that the slim, spiky-haired, leather-clad siren pictured on it was none other than her pal Melissa. She bought the album, took it home, and announced to Lauren: "I have just two words for you — Island Records." Then she put the album on. After hearing just a few notes, Lauren gasped, "Oh my God! Missy?!" As Lauren and Cindy explain, Melissa's style is very much the same today as it was back then, and the sound of her big 12-string Ovation is unmistakable.

At Melissa's invitation, Lauren and Cindy would often go to see Melissa entertain the big tippers at Ken's by George. Likewise, when Lauren performed several gigs at a place called 99's, Melissa went to see her. Lauren made a band demo tape with Melissa just before Melissa and her lover returned to Kansas. Melissa wrote guitar lead sheets for Lauren and her bass player, and Melissa's lover sang backup vocals. This woman was so incredibly shy, though, that she made everybody leave the room while she recorded her parts. The tunes they did were original Christian songs such as "There's a Way," "The Lord's Prayer," "Sand in My Shoes," and "Love One Another." Even some of Melissa's early riffs are similar to others she writes today, Cindy says. Overall, Lauren and Cindy feel that Melissa's music was not truly remarkable back then: they attribute her ultimate success to her determination and drive, not her musical talents. "She was relentless," Cindy comments. "She was like, 'I am going to be famous, and nothing is going to stand in my way.' " At Berklee, many people burned with a similar ambition.

During her college days, Melissa was a clown and an attention seeker — in short, a lot of fun to be around. Lauren loves to reminisce about the time Melissa lost her Berklee ID card and had to borrow someone else's in order to eat in the cafeteria. She was turned away because she didn't resemble the photo on the card, and, frustrated and hungry, she appealed to the dorm director for help. The director wrote her a note that read, "Please let Missy Etheridge eat!" It actually did the trick. Lauren also remembers that she and Cindy once stayed at Melissa and her lover's apartment for an entire weekend, from a Friday to a Sunday night. All day Sunday, they watched a Jerry Lewis movie marathon on TV. They would frequently get together to watch episodes of M*A*S*H*, too, or go for long walks and talk about their relationships.

Lauren recollects, also, that Melissa was ready to burst with excitement after meeting Bette Midler, whom, along with Bruce Springsteen, she absolutely adored. It was 26 September 1980, and the Divine Miss M. was in Boston for a book signing. Melissa and her lover showed up with a child the latter was sitting — a baby named Harrison. They received special attention from the star because Midler was dying to hold little Harrison.

Melissa and her lover were with Lauren and Cindy the night John Lennon was shot. This, though, is an occasion they remember with sadness, partly because Melissa and her partner could not understand what their friends were so upset about. Not being such huge fans of the Beatles, Melissa and her lover were taken aback when Lauren and Cindy wanted to spend the time mourning, not eating the pizza they'd just brought over.

Another sad memory for Lauren and Cindy is the slow

deterioration of Melissa's relationship with her girlfriend. It was not really in Melissa's nature to live her life ambivalently; the four would often talk longingly about what it would be like to acknowledge publicly the relationships they were in. Yet, as Christians, they were barely able to acknowledge the nature of their relationships to themselves. Melissa's lover still had an "official" boyfriend back in Kansas, but Melissa wanted to be out. She longed to explore her sexuality and her attraction to other women. This, Lauren feels, is what finally led to her utter disenchantment with traditional Christianity. Organized religion lacked the flexibility to embrace a young woman who needed to identify herself as a lesbian, privately and to the world.

Several times towards the end of Melissa's stay in Boston, her girlfriend called Lauren and Cindy late at night, worried that Melissa hadn't come home after her gig at Ken's by George. They later found out that Melissa had started to frequent Prelude's, a neighborhood gay club. The truth leaked out after Melissa went home with another woman one night and wrote a song about the experience. She played it for Lauren and Cindy at about three or four one morning when they were all exhausted. She concluded the performance by saying, "Okay, now I'm gonna 'fess up." The time was ripe for this confession because she had finally become entangled in the web of lies she had created to deceive her lover about her whereabouts. In any case, by this time she had lost all credibility.

While sharing her memories of this time, Cindy made a point of saying that the song Melissa played for them was "really touching," and that she was sure she would recognize it if she heard it again. On a hunch, I sent her a bootleg of a 1989 Bottom Line performance that includes a song Melissa claims to have written when she was nineteen years old. Cindy immediately identified it as that late-night confession piece. It's called "Ready to Love."

Lauren and Cindy are proud of Melissa for coming out and happy that she has achieved such enormous success as a singer-songwriter. They are pleased to see that these days lots of women, many of them inspired by Melissa, are choosing to pursue music careers. And they are particularly proud of Melissa for handling her fame so well. When Melissa began "publishing pictures of herself and her lover," she elicited even more admiration from her two old friends: those photos represent quite a breakthrough, they insist.

★　★　★

In April of 1981, Melissa and her girlfriend said goodbye to historic Boston and headed home. Etheridge remained in the Leavenworth area for a little over a year, playing such places as the Lavaranda Lounge at the Granada Royale Hotel in Kansas City; her last gig in Leavenworth had been at the Ramada Inn. Her goal, which she never lost sight of, was to scrape together enough money to buy her first car. This accomplished, she would drive straight to Los Angeles and get down to business. When she had the money, Melissa went to a used-car lot and settled on a yellow Mercury LN7. Although it was an ugly vehicle, it was the only one on the lot equipped with air conditioning, and Melissa realized that she'd be trekking across the desert on the way to L.A. (Schoemer). (One source has it that the car was actually a 1964 Impala, the so-called "blue Chevrolet" Etheridge refers to in the song "Nowhere to Go" [Zollo].)

During this year of preparation for a new life, Melissa adopted a vice that she hadn't previously felt the need for. She had taken to hanging out in Kansas City women's bars because, she discovered, "the only place you could meet other gay people [back then] was in a bar. And the worst thing in the world is to sit in a bar alone, right? So a cigarette could be your best friend." A short while later, when she found she couldn't sing because of a newly acquired smoker's cough, Etheridge thought, "OK, no matter how lonely I am, I have to sing." She promptly hurled the cigarettes into the trash, and hasn't touched them since.

About a week before Melissa was due to leave for Los Angeles, she came out to her parents, and, much to her relief, it was actually a positive experience. She told her father that she had something important about herself to share with him, and made sure he was sitting down. Terrified, he begged her to enlighten him. When Melissa announced that she was gay, her father was visibly relieved. "Is that all?" he said ("Melissa Etheridge: LN's Exclusive Interview"). "They knew anyway," Melissa now concedes. "It was very obvious. Very clear. They were fine. You know, long as I'm happy. That sort of thing" (qtd. in Phoenix). Elizabeth Etheridge has this to say about it all: "I didn't quite know how to deal with it." But, "I saw how lovely her friends were and how happy she was, and that's always been my main concern" (qtd. in Castro and Griffiths).

Melissa left for Los Angeles, alone, on her twenty-first birthday. It took her four days to make it to the city of her dreams. On the brink of departure, she tried to persuade a Kansas City bartender to go with her: "I remember being alone in a women's bar a week before I left," she says. "I was having some drinks and the bartender was looking really good, as they do sometimes. I was trying to convince her to come to L.A. with me and telling her I was going to be a famous rock star. She was going, 'Yea, right honey'" (qtd. in Aizlewood).

Three

HOTEL CALIFORNIA

Los Angeles was a jolt. If Berklee had been a jazz haven, then L.A., in the early 1980s, was a heavy-metal and glitter-rock pressure cooker. Arriving in June of 1982, Etheridge spent several weeks scouring the terrain for gigs with mounting desperation. Stringently budgeting her tiny cash reserves, she crashed at her aunt's place in Hollywood's bohemian Silverlake district.

At last, her diligence was modestly rewarded: "My first music job in L.A. was playing at the Candy Store on the east end of the Sunset Strip. . . . I went down to their showcase night, not knowing that the Candy Store was a black club. But I was accepted OK. They asked me back, and I played there for a few weeks — anything from Janis Joplin to Fleetwood Mac. George Benson's version of 'On Broadway' was popular then; I remember doing that" (qtd. in Everett).

Melissa soon discovered that it was even hard to make a living playing the more popular L.A. clubs. Lotus Land was crawling with musicians all bent on being discovered; many would play for free just to get a gig — or even pay for the privilege of being included in a showcase. Etheridge couldn't even get an audition at the Natural Fudge Company, a health-food restaurant in Hollywood (Zollo). She did, however, get the chance to try out for a job as a singing waitress: "It was at a place called the Great American Burger Co., I think. It was a family wedding. This little girl looked at me and stuck out her tongue" (qtd. in Dunn). It came to Etheridge at this point that she was not going to be able to keep her head above water in L.A. She just couldn't compete. Having pawned many of her possessions, still determined to support herself with her music, she found her way to the women's bars in Long Beach, Pomona, Pasadena, and Altadena, and here carved herself a comfortable niche in which she would hole up for the next six years.

Reflecting on how she wound up playing the women's-bar circuit in the first place, Etheridge remarks that during this period she found herself sitting in a Long Beach bar, "and, noticing a piano in the corner, talked myself into a gig, playing from 5 to 9, before the disco started. It worked into a situation where people were coming in to see *me*" (qtd. in Everett). The club in question was probably the Executive Suite. Dana Brown, who met Melissa in 1982 and remained friends with her until Dana moved away from the area in 1986, recalls Melissa playing there. The Executive Suite was a mixed bar on the Pacific Coast Highway that pulled in a significant number of very young women; it was often referred to by insiders as "Executive Sluts" or "Executive Sweat." Late on Sunday afternoons, Etheridge would infuse the club with a mellow atmosphere, serenading the crowd with piano ballads. Sensitive to market demand, she was fashioning herself more as a lounge act than a rock singer. Her instincts were right on. She gained a substantial following at this venue — Dana herself included. Melissa was even popular enough to pose for a

Rare publicity shot from 1983–84
DANA BROWN / RED SNAPPER PRODUCTIONS

*Rare publicity shot
from 1983–84*
DANA BROWN / RED
SNAPPER PRODUCTIONS

picture that Dana, a graphic artist, included in a women's calendar she was putting together. Despite Etheridge's appeal, Dana says, the management at Executive Suite eventually let her go, and so she and her following moved on to a new Long Beach watering hole, the Que Sera Sera, where she gigged regularly — once a week. Later she was asked to perform twice weekly.

Robbie's became another regular Etheridge venue, as did Vermie's in Pasadena, where they used to pass around a coffee can for tips. Driving home from Vermie's in her yellow Mercury LN7, Melissa tapped out the song "Occasionally" on her steering wheel. Every now and then she would share her new songs with Dana and a few other friends. Dana's memory of these impromptu performances is still vivid, and she points out that a number of the tunes ended up on Melissa's debut album. Besides "Occasionally," these include "Watching You," "I Want You," and "Bring Me Some Water." Another song Melissa used to perform in those days was "Meet Me in the Back," which, to the delight of her old fans, finally appeared on her third album, *Never Enough*, though some of the lyrics were revised. The original second verse had the singer teasing the audience — suggesting that she might meet an unnamed "you" in the back of the club if she brought some candy. On *Never Enough*, these lines were altered to include a message about safe sex.

But it is the Que Sera Sera that is most often evoked by Melissa Etheridge history buffs. She was "discovered" there. The Que "was the weirdest-assed bar," says Dana. "If you combine your living room and your kitchen, then you have the Que." Dawn Soldan, who met Melissa at the Que and later became her friend, describes the club as having three rooms. Friends with the bouncer, Mary Ellen (or Beetle, as everyone called her), Dawn was able to get into the Que and even help out behind the bar when the

Que Sera

DIANE STYMA

Que Sera recruits Etheridge fans

AD FROM NEWSLETTER *LAVENDER WAVE*

owner wasn't there, despite the fact that she was underage. She says the front room contained a walk-up bar, which extended along the entire length of the wall. The back room housed the pool tables, and was very cramped: there was barely enough room for the players to shoot. Melissa performed in the cosy, carpeted center room, which had a fireplace and was furnished with soft chairs and sectional sofas. There was also a very small dance floor in this room, and perched at its perimeter was the DJ's booth. Dana Brown reminisces fondly about the original layout of the old Que. It exuded an atmosphere of intimacy, and everyone could see the performers: "It was like having your best friend play music for you and you could chat with your friends and laugh and joke." Early bootlegs from the Que bear this out; as Melissa plays, you can hear ice clinking in the background, and between songs the entertainer can be heard bantering with her audience.

But as Etheridge's popularity burgeoned, that "weirdest-assed" bar was in danger of bursting at the seams. It was time for a transformation. By purchasing a section of the building next door, the Que's owners were able to knock down a wall and enlarge the dance floor. The floor of the center room was tiled over, and the couches were hauled away. High black tables and stools were installed in their place. The walls were painted lavender, and art reproductions were hung throughout. Most of the Que's faithful clientele appeared pleased with the results: the old haunt now seemed pretty classy compared to most of the women's bars in the area.

Dawn Soldan says that in the new incarnation of the Que, Melissa performed in a three-by-five-foot corner space in the general vicinity of the door. She talks about the night Melissa inadvertently assisted in the redecoration: "they had put a tall, obnoxious vase with these long, thrashing-out-in-all-directions dried 'things' in it on the small table in [Melissa's] corner where she set her drink . . . and electronic tuner and such, and she fought with these sprigs of wheat, or whatever they were, threatening to poke her eye out every time she turned around." Finally, Dawn recounts, Etheridge "set her guitar down and announced, 'I don't want to hurt anyone's feelings, but can we move this? I just don't feel . . . safe,' and she picked the massive thing up and relocated it to the floor out of the way." The offending piece of decor was subsequently removed to another part of the club.

Melissa was adored at the Que. A pack of Que-based groupies followed her around, fleshing out the audience each time she performed at another club. One faction of Pomona fans regularly drove forty minutes to Long Beach to see Melissa play, and Dana Brown says she often left Long Beach at four o'clock on Friday afternoons to go and hear Melissa perform in Pomona. Etheridge didn't drink alcohol, and so her fans would buy her cranberry juice and 7-Up: the little table that stood beside her when she performed was typically crammed with ten or more of these concoctions. Dawn Soldan claims that it became an inside joke to see how many drinks could be lined up on the table by the night's end, and the ever-solicitous Melissa would do her best to take at least one sip from each.

Those nights she spent playing at Leavenworth country-and-western bars, where hard-drinking patrons were inclined to cap the evening with a good brawl, had had a lasting impact on the teenaged Etheridge. Excessive alcohol consumption has been deeply unappealing to her ever since. When she does decide to have a drink, though, tequila is one of her most frequent choices ("Melissa Etheridge: She's Not in Kansas Anymore"). And even then, says Debe Shively — who, as Debe Tutone, DJ'd at the Que before and after Melissa's performances and between sets — when she does decide to have a drink or two after her final set or show of the evening, she doesn't "overindulge *ever*. I can't remember a single episode when she let her guard down."

Among Melissa's many fans from this era, probably the most widely remembered was a woman named Lisa, whom everyone referred to as "the tambourine lady." Though well-intentioned, she was somewhat over-enthusiastic in her idolization of Melissa. Debe Shively maintains that Lisa came to see Etheridge every single night she played, and brought her tambourine along with her. Initially, Lisa would just provide accompaniment for one or two songs, but, Debe says, "The monster grew until it became a constant SCHICKA . . . SCHICKA . . . SCHICKA . . . SCHICKA . . . the whole time Melissa played." Que customers tolerated the interference for the longest time, Debe continues, because it was seen as "a form of artistic expression." Then Lisa began to exercise her free-dom of expression with every number — fast, slow, blues, rock, or love song. So it came as no great surprise, says Cathy Romero, another Que regular, that the tambourine finally became a marked instrument. One night, in the middle of a song, a frustrated listener got up, marched over to Lisa, snatched the tambourine out of her hand, and broke it over her own knee to the sound of scattered applause.

But Lisa doggedly replaced the fractured instrument, and, when that one was destroyed, yet another tambou-rine appeared. Dawn Soldan jokes, "It is possible [Lisa] had a whole slew of them in the trunk of her car." Before the Que was remodeled and extended into an adjacent storefront, that space housed a music store, so "the next tambourine was nary a footstep away, [which was] a good thing for Melissa too," says Dawn, because "I can't count how many guitar strings went flying during overzealous renditions of 'Like the Way I Do.'" Lisa once made the fatal error of leaving one of her precious tambourines on a table during a set break, and a group of women, Beetle the bouncer among them, grabbed it, rushed outside, clambered onto a bus-stop bench, and hurled the offending article onto the roof. "There was quite the brawl afterward," Dawn reminisces, "mostly the exchange of ugly words, and then [Lisa] pacing up and down in front of the bar cursing."

Did Lisa ever take the hint? Apparently not, because at one of Melissa's first real concerts — held at the Long Beach Arena — there was Lisa, up front in the aisle, tapping away on yet another tambourine. Yet no one recalls Melissa ever saying a negative word about the tambourine lady; as Dawn, among others, emphasizes, she cherished her fans. On a shopping expedition, Dawn ran across a button that read, "Toto, I don't think we're in Kansas anymore." She bought it on impulse, because it made her think of how Melissa must have felt leaving Leavenworth for a high-powered metropolis like Los Angeles. When she presented her find to Melissa, Etheridge hugged her and pinned the button to her guitar strap. "She was like that with all of us," Dawn says. "We were always giving her little things, but I believe she truly appreciated it."

On stage, Melissa established a rapport with her audience that virtually every member of the old Que crowd remarks upon. Dana Brown recalls that Melissa had a habit of picking out people she knew in the audience to tease; Dawn Soldan says that Beetle was frequently among the chosen. Etheridge liked to do a rendition of Leonard Cohen's hauntingly beautiful "Suzanne." The last verse contains the line, "There are heroes in the seaweed." Despite the song's solemn tone, Melissa would fix her eyes on Beetle and sing, "And there was Beetle in the seaweed," just to get the bouncer's attention. Regulars would fold dollar bills into airplanes and launch them at Melissa's tip jar, which she kept on the floor in front of her. "In the middle of a song [Melissa] had to dodge our incoming tip attacks, and try not to laugh," Dawn remembers. Over at Vermie's, audience members would toss their shoes (echoes of *Rocky Horror Picture Show* screenings) at Melissa during "I Want You," because she would slur the chorus, making it sound like she was singing "I want shoes." Of course, Etheridge was a shameless flirt. "Meet Me in the Back" was a showstopper: Melissa would arch her eyebrows at the women in the audience, toy with the buttons on her shirt, and incline her head towards the back door.

Playing at the women's bars of southern California not only schooled Etheridge in the methods of attracting and holding audience attention, but it also taught her quite a bit about songwriting. She has claimed (on Rockline) that it was in this milieu that she learned to write personal music. After fashioning a pop-hit kind of number, she'd think to herself, "They're really going to love this." But when the time came to perform it, the bar patrons would go on talking, drinking, and laughing — tuning her out. If she wrote a song that came from her heart and soul, she'd be fearful or embarrassed to play it, yet those were the songs that shut people up and held them in thrall. Those were the songs that were requested over and over again.

There are several Etheridge compositions that Melissa used to perform regularly at the Que and other area bars, songs that have to date not appeared on any of her albums. Dana Brown is convinced that a good many of them would be hits if Melissa would only record and release them. "Ready to Love," of course, is one. Another, "Dancing in the Fire," Dawn Soldan claims was inspired by the care instructions on the tag of some jeans Melissa had purchased. Other unrecorded originals include "Hearts and

All," "Love Song," "Angel," "Whispers My Heart," "You and I Know," "A Lot Like You," "I Don't Know" (which is alternately titled "I Don't Want to Hear It"), "Love Is Just a Giving Game," "Don't Look at Me," "Juliet, Where's Your Romeo?" "Lovin' a Stranger," "America," "Do You Want to Love Me," and "Over the Line."

Etheridge routinely performed a series of cover songs, as well, though over the years these were gradually replaced by original compositions. Springsteen's "I'm on Fire" and "Pink Cadillac" were audience favorites. Joan Armatrading provided first-rate material, too: Melissa did "Love and Affection," "The Weakness in Me," "Down to Zero," and "I Love It When You Call Me Names" (the tambourine lady would shout obscenities during this last one).

Upon arriving in California, Etheridge rediscovered Janis Joplin. During her VH-I Roots of Rock and Roll concert in 1994, she confessed she'd first seen Joplin perform on the *Ed Sullivan Show* when she was just eleven. Joplin "actually scared me," she reminisced: the sixties rocker seemed to be "all hair and screaming." But after she had grown up and learned about love, she found she could totally relate. According to Dawn Soldan, Melissa's closing set would often consist of three Joplin songs, including "Piece of My Heart" (during which she would break to recount a personal anecdote that changed with each retelling).

Melissa would close, on occasion, with a rousing, Bette Midler-esque rendition of "When a Man Loves a Woman" — except she would change the lyrics to "when a woman loves a woman." "We all got into it," Dawn recalls, "and she would go for almost a half hour on it sometimes, depending on how much we egged her on." Etheridge also covered James Taylor, Culture Club, Van Morrison, the Beatles (a band she'd learned to appreciate after her

college days), Cyndi Lauper, John Mellencamp, Hucy
Lewis and the News, Rickie Lee Jones, the Rolling Stones,
and even Elvis, among others.

Was Etheridge in those days the strong performer, the
immense talent, that she is today? To many there is no
doubt about it: the answer is a resounding "yes." Gabriela
Loza, who still lives in the area, remembers going with
friends to the Que to shoot pool and seeing Etheridge
perform for the first time. As her contingent was making
a beeline for the poolroom, Gabriela was caught up short.
A woman was playing guitar and belting out a song. "Right
away I was floored." After witnessing a few more performances, Gabriela found herself predicting great things for
that lone entertainer: "The amazing thing was, you kind
of knew she was going to make it . . . at least I knew."

But Paul Edie, himself a musician who sometimes
gigged in the Long Beach area — serving as a substitute
performer for various jazz combos in the evenings after
putting in a day's work as an engineer — says that at this
time Melissa's talent revealed itself only intermittently.
Paul saw her play maybe half a dozen times between 1983
and 1986, and on most of these occasions she seemed to
be performing at a "low groove." Knowing full well the
heights Etheridge was capable of reaching, Paul also
recounts what happened the first time he heard her play.
Romantically involved, at the time, with a woman who
was friends with a number of lesbians, Paul was comfortable frequenting such bars as Vermie's and Executive
Suite. One night, he and his lover went to such an establishment to catch a performer one of Paul's friends had
simply described as a Berklee College of Music graduate.
The first two sets were unremarkable; the songs, Paul says,
were "well-performed, but almost mechanical and very
uninspired." He mentions elevator music. Bored by these
offerings, the couple prepared to leave, but then Etheridge

returned for her third set and they lingered for a moment. "She kicked off a tune I had never heard," relates Paul. "It started quietly and built slowly. By the second verse, the talking in the bar had stopped. By the third, nobody was even moving. It was like everybody was frozen. Without attempting to sound overly dramatic, it blew my socks off." "I mean," he continues, "all of a sudden out of nowhere, this woman went from dull to super-intense. It was like somebody turned on a switch somewhere. And it didn't let up. The entire set was like that . . . there was this unexplainable energy that just exploded out of her."

Paul also happened to see Melissa perform at a benefit festival in 1984. He and the friend he had gone with were among the only men there. Though the concert itself was free, Paul threw a few dollars into a can someone was passing around. A number of women performed that day, and each played for about forty-five minutes, but in Paul's mind Melissa was in a league of her own. She galvanized the crowd after playing only a few bars. "I noticed for the first time that she was handling the guitar like it was a part of her act . . . not just as an instrument that was hanging from her neck," remarks Paul. "She could twist it and get this wild vibrato sound that was a kick. It was more like an extension of herself than it was an inanimate object . . . and God, could she play that thing. . . . She held the rhythm like a metronome . . . didn't rush and slow down in the middle of songs like some performers do, but constantly drove the music forward. She was not reacting to the beat, she was pushing it."

Of Melissa's voice that day, Paul had this to say: "I could not get over what she [could] do with her voice. Her pitch was *always* dead-on accurate. I never heard her slide flat or sharp . . . she could change the texture and mood of her voice in an instant and almost sound like two different women were singing. A raspy lower register that could

turn into an intense and piercing siren in a heartbeat."
Paul's friend was a bass player, and he was struck by
the purity of Etheridge's skill as forcefully as Paul was.
Melissa's original tunes were not cluttered with showy
guitar effects or complex counter-rhythms; she seldom
modulated keys where the listener would expect her to;
she tended to choose sharp keys, which, Paul says, in itself
lent a unique quality to her sound. He recalls that his
bass-playing friend announced in amazement: "She can
express more in a single song with five repetitive chords
than most bands can do in an entire set."

These peaks and dips in Etheridge's performance level
are attributable, according to Paul, more to the venue
factor than anything else: in a bar, a musician just cannot
command the full attention of the audience. Bar patrons
are there to drink, to mingle, to have a good time. Even
Melissa has wryly commented that during her Long Beach
days, she knew she was having a good night when the
bartender would wait to run the blender until after she'd
finished a song. It's much easier to perform for a stadium
audience of ten thousand people, she told an Australian
television interviewer, than it is to play in front of fifteen
drunken revellers. When she ventured to appear anywhere
other than the area women's bars, Melissa was just another
Long Beach musician — nothing special. It had to have
gotten to her, at least at times, Paul insists: she would sit
there hour after hour, night after night, playing for people
who couldn't care less about what she was trying to communicate. An audience-centered performer, Etheridge
needed to sense a steady stream of energy coming from
the crowd in order to sizzle on stage. Melissa does concede
that she began to feel she was reaching the end of her
tether: she craved a record deal that steadfastly refused to
materialize. "I was like, 'God, what am I *doing*? This is
going to take *forever*'" (qtd. in Schoemer).

Cathy Romero, who saw Melissa perform only at the comfortable, supportive Que, agrees with Paul Edie: Melissa's performance level did have its mountains and valleys. Even in her natural element — the women's bars — Melissa would have some "off nights." On these occasions, Cathy observes, Etheridge seemed to be "in her own world."

But it was always clear that Melissa wanted to make it. She'd pulled up stakes and migrated to California to become famous, and she was determined to scale the heights of the business, whatever it took. It appeared, for awhile, that it might take shifting her sights to television. In 1982, Etheridge was hired to do an episode of *Fantasy*, a daytime show hosted by Leslie Uggams and Peter Marshall. She sang "On Broadway," and later admitted that she had been "dreadful" ("It's Melissa"). Next, she enhanced the pilot episode of *I Had 3 Wives*, a detective show featuring a male investigator whose three wives constantly butt into his work and, much to his annoyance, always manage to solve the case before he does. The pilot revolves around a murder that has been committed in a Santa Monica club, and Melissa, along with a network-assembled band, is the house entertainment. As far as Dawn Soldan remembers, Melissa and her crew were relegated to the background, though they did get to perform two original Etheridge compositions: "You and I Know" and "Precious Pain."

In 1984, Melissa auditioned for the hit television series *Fame*. Ken Ehrlich, *Fame*'s supervising producer, remarks that her audition was strong: Etheridge "was stunning, really terrific, and actually not bad in terms of line reading. I was looking that year for more of a rock 'n' roll edge to the show, and I thought that she could have done that" (qtd. in Everett). But she lost the part to Janet Jackson.

Dana Brown's take on the *Fame* audition is more illuminating, though. At the time, Dana was dating a woman named Sarah, who happened to be the assistant music director for *Fame*. Dana encouraged Sarah to come down to the Que one night to hear Melissa perform. Sarah did, and was so impressed that she had Melissa moved to the head of the audition list. When the big day arrived, a nervous Dana drove a calm Melissa to the audition. Melissa marched right in, stretched out her hand, and said, "Hi, I'm Melissa Etheridge, and I'm here to . . . blah, blah, blah." Dana smiles at the memory of her friend's extraordinary confidence. She watched the audition, for which Melissa did one Elvis song and one of her own. "She was great," Dana says simply. Immediately afterwards, Dana stepped outside for a moment: a long line of *Fame* hopefuls stretched down the block and out of sight. Back inside, she discovered that Melissa had been asked to read from a script. While her reading was going on, Dana eavesdropped on some other auditions. They were awful. It was clear to Dana that Melissa was a shoo-in.

That night, everyone congregated at Vermie's. Melissa, buzzing with excitement over the day's events, neglected to thank either Dana or Sarah. Dana says she shrugged off this oversight — it was no big deal, Melissa was quite justifiably on a high, and it had just slipped her mind — but Sarah couldn't do the same. "That does it!" she said. An absolute stickler when it came to people maintaining their humility, Sarah found Melissa's perceived ingratitude to be unforgivable. If *Fame* was going to be saddled with a prima donna, then it should at least be a *well-known* one. With a touch of wistfulness in her voice, Dana remarks that Melissa would surely have been invited to join the cast of *Fame* if she'd only remembered to say thanks . . . but of course, as Ken Ehrlich points out, "Not being hired was perhaps the best thing that could have happened to Melissa . . . for a music career, other than Janet's, it wasn't necessarily the right place to be" (qtd. in Everett).

If inadvertently offending the show's assistant music director hadn't been enough to scuttle Etheridge's chances, another factor might have done the trick. Melissa had acquired a manager, Bill Leopold, best known at the time for his work with the group Bread. Dana Brown explains that the *Fame* brass preferred to deal directly with the artists themselves. When Melissa won the chance to audition, she had no representation but by the time the audition rolled around, Leopold was on board; this likely contributed to Sarah's impression that Etheridge was a woman with an attitude. Yet Leopold's sudden arrival on the scene may have been entirely coincidental, and, quite simply, the result of a good business decision.

The Etheridge-Leopold connection was actually a marriage made in heaven, despite its unremarkable beginnings: Melissa had a friend who played soccer (or softball, according to some sources) with a friend of Leopold's wife. A demo tape of Melissa's was passed along this chain to Leopold, and he liked what he heard. While some artists change managers on an almost annual basis, Melissa Etheridge and Bill Leopold are still rocking steady after more than a decade. Leopold has always respected the fact that Melissa is a lesbian, and in those early days did not try to talk her into playing the straight bars as a means of making herself more appealing to the major record labels. He had no trouble at all persuading label reps to venture out to the women's bars where they could catch Etheridge live. It was the best strategy Leopold could have adopted: these intimate venues fostered Melissa's best performances — in them she was loved, and in them she shone. And ultimately the strategy worked.

Don Zimmerman, a good friend of Leopold's and president of Capitol Records, was the first to act on Leopold's suggestion. He saw Melissa perform several times, and then brought a few other Capitol people along to hear her.

Zimmerman and producer John Carter were favorably impressed; other members of their party felt her original songs were too introspective. But certainly, Zimmerman comments, Melissa "wasn't introspective in terms of her performance" (qtd. in Everett). Zimmerman decided to finance a few demos. "It was a big deal at the Que," Cathy Romero says as she reminisces about the night Melissa brought in the first demo and had it played over the sound system. The excitement was ephemeral, however. Etheridge was to go no further with Capitol Records because Zimmerman left shortly thereafter to take a position with EMI International in London (Everett).

Etheridge's prospects weren't totally squelched by this setback, though: connections had been made. John Carter, who left Capitol for A & M, brought along one of the Etheridge demos he'd produced and played it for Lance Freed, president of A & M's publishing operation. The label wasn't interested in issuing a recording contract, but Freed did want to know if Etheridge was interested in signing on as a songwriter. "I wasn't sure about her songs," Freed now concedes, "but I went to [a] bar in Altadena and heard Melissa sing. Live music was just an excuse for people to talk louder in that club, but Melissa and her 12-string just took over and commanded the room. She and I had lunch at Hampton's on LaBrea and I offered her a staff writing job" (qtd. in Everett).

There was no need to ask twice. Melissa penned songs three days per week in A & M's offices and was rewarded with a regular paycheck. Freed came to believe that Melissa had an inherent talent for songwriting but still needed to polish her skills. She could not write collaboratively or custom fit her material to the musical styles of other artists, but, Freed asserts, "if she wanted to write for a particular project, she could do it with just a little distraction. If someone want[ed] a particular sentiment in a song, she [could] deliver it.'' The best advice Freed ever gave Etheridge was to practice greater self-discipline: '' 'Keep it simple' — 'Say what you mean' — and she got very good at that'' (qtd. in Everett).

So, for two and a half years, Melissa held down a day job and played the bars at night. A & M presented her demos to various record companies, but although Melissa's voice was universally admired, nobody was ready to sign her. Etheridge was assigned by A & M to create songs for movie soundtracks, and by so doing, the company managed to see a good return on their investment in her. Among the best known is the soundtrack for the 1987 Nick Nolte film *Weeds*, which is about a group of ex-convicts who try to make it in the outside world by putting on a musical. Melissa penned four songs for this film, one of them with Orville Stoeber, and was also asked to teach Nolte how to sing them for the movie.

Etheridge had an active personal life, as well. She lived for a while with a group of women and also had a series of short-lived relationships. The old crowd remember Melissa's romantic partners only vaguely. At one point she was with a woman who had long, dark hair and wire-rimmed glasses; this woman would wear flower-print skirts and sit by the door to the Que with Beetle. There was also the drummer who played with Melissa at the 1983 Women's Music Festival in Long Beach. For a few short months, Melissa had a lover who was cute and hilariously funny. She had another affair with a member of a women's band she toured with on the women's-bar and festival circuit.

Melissa was an object of desire for many women, and, in turn, often found herself attracted to others. Monogamy was out of the question for her, and she embarked on and abandoned quite a few relationships. Etheridge admits as much today, declaring that Julie Cypher, her current

lover, is the only person to whom she has ever been completely faithful. Musing on the emotional landscape of her
early-twenties self, she concludes that "Lust is just searching — I think as human beings we are searching for, you
know, what's gonna make us feel better, what's gonna take
that pain away. And, um, a lot of people go drinking and
taking drugs to try to numb the pain. I found it in physical
relationships." She hadn't yet developed the vital capacity
for self-sufficiency that we all require to maintain an
even emotional keel: "the things that were missing, that I
hadn't found in myself yet, that I couldn't fill up in myself
. . . I [looked] for someone else to fill them up" (qtd. in
Phoenix). The lesbian crowd Etheridge ran with was, not
surprisingly, a little on the wild side — probably more a
symptom of age than anything else. "Sure, I went through
some wild periods," says Melissa. "I'd say my early twen-
ties were pretty crazy. But I was always conscious in the
craziness. I mean, I got messed up, absolutely," but never
did she succumb to the drug use or excessive drinking so
often linked to the after-hours world she was exploring
(Zollo).

Paul Edie, who'd had a brush with the bisexual and
lesbian scenes, contends, however, that "wild" is too tame
a word for Melissa and her cohorts in those early days —
and he is not talking about drug use or torrid love affairs.
He explains that at the time an atmosphere of repression
pervaded the gay and lesbian community of Long Beach.
It was, fundamentally, a question of survival. The largest
local employer was an aerospace company, and nearby
were other major aerospace companies, such as Hughes,
Northrop, and Rockwell. Many of these corporations sub-
jected prospective employees to a security clearance, and
in those days homosexuality was adequate justification for
denying such clearance, and, therefore, employment. It
was also not uncommon, Paul continues, for the federal

government to submit its own employees to random security checks; one tactic the feds utilized was to drop by the gay bars to see who was there; such investigations were usually triggered by a tip from a coworker. "This," says Paul, "resulted in a really hidden gay culture in the area."

"But for reasons I can't explain," he elaborates, "the [gay] women . . . went bonkers late at night." They'd drive around hooting and hollering, throwing kisses to other women, and drenching unsuspecting pedestrians with big squirt guns. After midnight, the feds generally packed it in, and at the witching hour many of the gay women Paul was acquainted with, "who I knew as professional managers and engineers, who would never dream of coming out, would run around in these small gangs dressed in all the black leather and metal buttons, and get nuts." Early one morning he was shopping at a Safeway store when a mob of these women stormed in. Some piled into vacant grocery carts and their sisters raced with those carts up and down the aisles, crashing into things and hassling straight customers — this latter action involved bombarding poor Paul with stale rolls.

It's unclear whether Melissa ever engaged in any such decompression antics, but Paul explains that resentment grew in certain sectors of the gay and lesbian community towards these women, referred to by some as the "wilders." "There was this ongoing battle between those who participated and those who did not," Paul says, explaining that the more conservative lesbians he knew felt the wilders gave the gay community a bad name. Some felt so strongly about this that even though they knew Melissa was a local hero and an excellent musician, they refused to support her because of her "reputation as a 'wilder.'" You could spot the wilders right away: they wore tight black leather and shiny stretch pants. "There was a new generation of lesbians coming out who learned to rock and to dance,"

Melissa has said. "We weren't into folk music, women's-music stuff. We wore silly metallic clothing, we stayed out all night." But despite that palpable sense of being party to the inception of a whole new cultural mode, Melissa is adamant that she "wouldn't go back [to those days] for anything. . . . It's nice to have experienced it and be out of it" ("Melissa Etheridge: In through the Out Door").

Another Paul Edie story demonstrates beautifully how Melissa's essential humanity still easily penetrated the radical alienation that fueled the scene she was moving in. One night he found himself sharing a table with about twelve women, including his girlfriend, while watching Etheridge perform. During a set break, Etheridge came and sat down at their table to chat with one of the women, a friend. Paul, parked at the opposite end of the table, wasn't really paying attention to the conversation, and suddenly he was smacked with a projectile wadded-up napkin. The women at the far end of the table, including Melissa, all had their eyes on him. They were laughing.

Paul braced himself for the verbal onslaught he knew was coming: "What the hell is a guy doing in here, any-way?" "Why don't you wait outside on your leash?" "Men are only good for one thing." Melissa, Paul says, was right in there pitching; she kept the one-liners coming. Her zingers, he now says, would "probably make pretty good joke-book material" — full of sexual innuendo. When it was established that Paul was the significant other of one of the women at the table, his tormentors backed off and left him alone.

But then two of the women entered into a heated debate about men and their relative uselessness. This turned nasty, and some heavy swearing and name calling ensued. At this point, Melissa and a few others, including Paul and his partner, left the table. A short while later, while Paul was at the bar, Melissa approached him "by herself, and kind of sheepishly told me that she hoped I did not take all those jokes personally . . . and that she appreciated my ability to laugh at myself. I never forgot the fact that she took the time and went out of her way to make that comment." And then she went back to her stool and started her next set.

Was there a genuine split in the les/bi/gay community over the issue of the wilders? It depends on who you ask. Many don't concede that there was ever a problem. They insist that Long Beach was anything *but* a repressive community back then. Lorna Albertsen graced that scene clad in leather and the obligatory metallic stretch pants simply because "that was stylish then." The wilders, she maintains, were just young women having fun and "not hurting anyone, except ourselves at times." They may have whooped at other women from car windows, but they were, fundamentally, feminists and political activists. Lorna was president of the Long Beach Lambda Democratic Club for three years and attended the 1984 Democratic National Convention in San Francisco. In Long Beach, she points out, there was a gay and lesbian community center that sponsored a number of annual events; there was a newsletter, *The Lavender Wave*, published by a group of women who held big community picnics every year; and there was even an annual gay-pride march.

Melissa was supportive of local gay and lesbian political efforts. Lorna had organized a Blood Sisters Blood Drive in Long Beach based on one that had been mounted in San Diego. For several Wednesdays in a row, she set up camp at the door of the Que, and from this strategic location worked hard to recruit women donors. Melissa contributed in her own way, Lorna says, "by using that fabulous voice of hers and announcing the 'Blooooood Sisters' being there." (Incidentally, when Lorna was preparing to go to San Francisco for the Democratic National Convention, the Que sponsored a fundraiser for her.) Sensitive to Lorna's political commitment, Melissa, the night after Ronald Reagan's 1984 reelection, "shared her disappointment" with Lorna "from the stage." Lorna hasn't forgotten.

Etheridge's involvement with the women's community also overlapped, at least for a while, with her musical aspirations. When she first arrived in Los Angeles, she sent a demo recording to Olivia Records, a women's music label, but she was turned down. She also played some of the women's music festivals, such as Robin Tyler's West Coast Women's Music and Comedy Festival, where she met and made a great impression on women's music icon Alix Dobkin. Alix evokes that meeting with a revealing anecdote. Immediately after the festival, Alix was slated to tour southern California. She had to get right on the road in a rented car, but, much to her chagrin, "suddenly the rental companies required a credit card, and I didn't have one." In desperation, she presented her dilemma to some of the other women playing the festival. Melissa promptly offered to lend Alix her MasterCard. After the festival, the two hooked up at a Los Angeles rental office. She "charged the car to her account," Alix says, "and told me not to worry about it but to pay her back when I could. Neither of us had much money. When my tour was over I returned the car and settled up with [Melissa] in cash."

But Alix also observes that Melissa was not universally embraced by women's music aficionados. On one occasion, Etheridge provoked consternation among certain members of her audience by covering Joan Armatrading's "I Love It When You Call Me Names": the song's sadomasochistic theme was not to their taste. In this era, women's music was charting a course for itself that it was not in Etheridge's nature to follow: "I was always rock 'n' roll, whereas their music was quieter, more folky" (qtd. in Everett). Still, after hearing Melissa perform for the first time, Robin Tyler predicted, "She will be a star. She's tremendously gifted." "She reminded me some of Janis Joplin," Robin recalls — "the energy without the self-destruction. She sang from her gut" (qtd. in Etheridge, "Melissa Etheridge: LN's Exclusive Interview"). Holly Near, one of the biggest names in women's music since the 1970s, says that when she heard Melissa perform, her immediate reaction was *Oh, no, another girl with a guitar. But she was tearing them up. She ended with a Janis Joplin classic and did it no discredit"* (qtd. in Gaar).

In light of such glowing endorsements as these, it seems the persistent rumor that the women's music community wholly rejected Melissa doesn't really pan out. It is true that the thorny issue of political correctness has reared up and jabbed at Etheridge. She describes how this happened, on one occasion, just as she was trying to establish a rapport — a point of personal identification — with a women's music festival audience: "I talked about being with a girl and having her leave me and what I went through — gaining ten pounds and stuff like that," Melissa recalls. "Well, after the concert I literally had to hold off all these women who were saying that the songs I sang were all about abuse and that the comment I had made about being ten pounds overweight was terrible and that they were going to come string me up. It was my first PC call, you know. I realized, *Oh, there's so many things I have to be aware of"* ("Melissa: Rock's Great Dyke Hope"). Are there ever.

Yet, as Alix Dobkin insists, Melissa had many admirers in that scene. Melissa, she points out, "has still not forgotten who she is or the women's music she comes from." Alix's message to Melissa is simple and forthright and effectively overrides all the negativity and factionalism: "We're so proud of you," Alix says.

Four

STAR ASCENDING

Looking, to Melissa, "like a derelict off Venice Beach," Chris Blackwell shambled into the Que Sera Sera one night late in 1986 (qtd. in Aizlewood). Sporting beach pants, his flip-flops slapping the floor as he wended his way through the crowd, Blackwell was late: only four songs were left in Melissa's set. Despite appearances, this man was no derelict. Blackwell was the founder of Island Records. He had made Bob Marley a reggae superstar and discovered Irish rockers U2. And the four songs hit their mark: after the set, Etheridge says, Blackwell sought her out and announced, "I like your songs. I like your presence, and I'm very intrigued." He also drove home his conviction that the future of rock and roll had a female face ("Melissa Etheridge," *Us*).

Blackwell traces the chain of events that led him to the Que that night. "A guy named Dino Airali rang me one day," he recalls. "I'd just been to Sacramento, seeing some groups, and nothing was happening there, and I was leaving Los Angeles the next day." Airali, who had produced Phoebe Snow's first album, told Blackwell that an artist he'd cut a demo with would be performing that night at a Long Beach club. Concerned about making it back to Los Angeles in time for a meeting he'd set for later that night, Blackwell asked Airali how long it would take them to drive to Long Beach. "Twenty minutes," was the response, and so the music hounds set out on yet another hunting expedition. "Of course," says Blackwell, "it took an hour to get there, and I walked into this club in which, to my surprise, Dino and I were the only men. At first I felt that I might not be welcome, but I figured out very quickly that, as the record company guy, I had a reason to be there" (qtd. in Everett).

The resulting Etheridge-Blackwell encounter has produced a fair measure of mutual admiration. Says Melissa: "He saw the same [thing] as the audience and that's what makes him a great music man. He was touched by the performance, the songs, the soul, the reality" (qtd. in Aizlewood). Blackwell claims that he "was amazed, to tell you the truth, that somebody of this obvious sort of strength had not been signed by anybody" (qtd. in Etheridge, "Melissa Etheridge: LN's Exclusive Interview").

On the spot, Blackwell was ready to sign Melissa to his label. But Melissa was skeptical. After all, she had come so close so often — with Capitol, with A & M, with Warner Brothers, with EMI — that part of her just could not accept that her dream was finally coming true. At least until she saw a contract. And even then, "Just 'cause you get a record contract, that doesn't guarantee you'll ever make a record. And even if you make a record, that doesn't guarantee it will be released. And even if it's released, that doesn't guarantee anyone will hear it" (qtd. in Rogovoy). But Blackwell came through. He came a second time to see Melissa play with some other Island people in tow. His lawyers started drawing up the papers.

Rolling Stone interviewer Rich Cohen, after hearing her

recount the "magical" tale of how she came to sign with
Island Records, asked: "So at that point did your life just
turn around? Did you call your parents and say, 'Thanks
for the guitar lessons, I'm a rock star?' " But in the real
world, such turnarounds are rare. "You know, it's funny,"
Etheridge mused. "You get signed, and you think, 'Oh,
that's it.' But, no, I played at the bar, still had to make a
living. Chris Blackwell went back to Jamaica or the Baha-
mas or London or wherever he went to. I had to make a
record."

Alix Dobkin went to see Melissa play at the Que right
after she'd signed the Island contract but before she'd
recorded her first album. Touring southern California to
bolster her own fourth album, *Never Been Better*, Alix had
her daughter Adrian and a few friends with her. As she was
only sixteen at the time, Adrian was barred from the club,
so Alix and her pals took turns waiting with Adrian out on
the street until Melissa's last set was over. "Rather than
hanging out at the bar," says Alix, "Melissa left immediately so that all of us could go out for ice cream together."
Despite having been "discovered" and signed to a mainstream label, Melissa treated Adrian as a peer when she
discussed her record project with the group. Melissa, Alix
remembers, "expressed her determination not to sell out
and to do it her way, which was exactly what happened.
We were all very excited for her and I told her that I
knew she would be a big star. She received the prediction
humbly without any attitude or illusions of grandeur."

How often do these things work out as planned? The
debut album, *Melissa Etheridge*, is *not* the first Melissa
recorded. The first consisted of ten original songs
recorded in San Francisco and produced by Jim Gaines,
who had also worked with the likes of Huey Lewis and
the News, Journey, and Eddie Money. Typical of the time,
this album was recorded in layers: first rhythm, then many

levels of instrumentation, including synthesizers and drum machines, and, finally, the voice — almost as an afterthought. The finished product sounded more like A Flock of Seagulls than Melissa Etheridge. On VH-I's *Two Dollar Stare*, Melissa remarked (a little sheepishly): "When I went in to make my first album . . . it was myself. Solo. And we put together musicians, a producer was assigned . . . I had never made an album before and I didn't act like I knew how to do it. I was very insecure. So I let things get out of my creative control. And it wasn't me." On another occasion she elaborated: "I was a solo artist, and it's very hard to just go in and say, 'OK, I'm going to make my music.' I had never played with a group; I had never made a record before. The first thing record companies do is hook you up to a producer," and, Etheridge continues, the first thing that producer does is put his or her personal "stamp on your music. The first producer's sound was not compatible to my sound. It became over-produced, it wasn't intimate" (qtd. in Tomlinson).

Fortunately, Chris Blackwell hated it. "What I wanted," he now explains, "was something as close as possible to what I had seen and, frankly, all I had seen was her and a guitar. While I didn't want to make a record with just a guitar, I didn't want a group image — I just wanted to hear her" (qtd. in Everett). An album-cover photo had already been taken — Melissa in jeans and a leather jacket, head thrown back, fists raised, ferociously alive against a back-drop of solid, blazing red — and Blackwell taped it to the studio wall. He then ordered all concerned (according to Melissa's old A & M boss, Lance Freed) "to make the album that goes with that picture" (qtd. in Everett). Melissa was powerfully relieved: Blackwell was going to finance a recut.

While cutting a demo, Melissa had met drummer Craig Krampf; he, in turn, introduced her to bassist Kevin

McCormick. Kevin, a talented musician, said to Melissa, "Look, we can make this album together. Your songs are straightforward. They're easy to record. All we need is four days" (qtd. in Etheridge, "Melissa Etheridge: In through the Out Door"). He was right. Melissa Etheridge's eponymous debut album was recorded live in studio with three primary musicians: McCormick on bass, Krampf on drums, and Etheridge on her acoustic twelve-string. A few session musicians were called in for over-dubbing work on some cuts: Waddy Wachtel and Johnny Lee Schell on guitar; Scott Thurston and Wally Badarou on keyboards. The disk was produced by Krampf, McCormick, Etheridge, and engineer Niko Bolas. Everyone was pleased with the pared-down end product — including main man Blackwell. In her liner notes, Melissa proffered thanks to (naturally) Blackwell; Bill Leopold; her parents; her sister; her nephew and niece; her lover, Kathleen; and Mary Ellen, a.k.a. Beetle, the bouncer from the Que.

Longtime fans and new converts alike select *Melissa Etheridge* and its follow-up, *Brave and Crazy*, as their favorites. Appearing in 1996 on *VH-1 Duets* — a television show in which a guest artist performs several of her own compositions with another singer (and vice versa) — Etheridge was paired with Joan Osborne and with Paula Cole, among others. Melissa's debut album, at that point about ten years old, was the compilation of choice: Osborne put dibs on "Bring Me Some Water," and Cole claimed "Occasionally." The first album also contains Melissa's signature anthem, "Like the Way I Do," written in 1985 about a woman with whom Etheridge was having an affair who proceeded to become involved with someone else while still seeing Etheridge. It's the tune Melissa likes to perform best: the consummate lyric of anguished, undignified, outraged, lay-it-all-out-on-the-table jealousy; its unique, scratchy rhythm mimics the action of something eating

*Melissa and
Sophie B. Hawkins
From* VH-1 Duets,
Doheny Mansion, L.A.
NEAL PRESTON / RETNA

away at your insides, especially as Etheridge screams the chorus. Sometimes, when performing solo, she adds percussion by slapping the face of her guitar. When Etheridge does "Like the Way I Do" in concert (often drawing it out to last ten minutes or more), the effect on the crowd is dynamic: the responsive energy she creates down on the floor snaps and crackles. There's always a point when she and the audience reach a plateau, and the performance becomes almost an out-of-body experience for her. She has described the effect many times to interviewers. She has to take a deep breath to ground herself again.

The album's most famous cut, however, is another rocker, "Bring Me Some Water," based on an open relationship Etheridge was involved in and having difficulty handling. In the song, she says she knows her lover is human and can't condemn her for her infidelity. After an intensifying series of eighth-note downstrums, the song explodes into the chorus — the singer's plea for mercy. She begs for water because she's "burning alive" with jealousy: her lover is in the throes of passion with somebody else.

Of the three singles released from *Melissa Etheridge* in the United States — "Similar Features," "Like the Way I Do," and "Bring Me Some Water" — the latter received the most radio airplay and was the song Etheridge performed at the televised 1989 Grammy Awards ceremony. It was also the focal point of a 1996 article in *Acoustic Guitar* magazine. From a guitar perspective, the writer declares, " 'Bring Me Some Water' is [a] standout tune. In the verse riff, [Etheridge] plays A notes on three consecutive string courses and then does the same thing with D; because she's playing a 12-string, six strings are chiming the same note in three different octaves. This is a very nice use of the unique qualities of the 12-string, and it brings a new twist to the old faithful I-IV-V structure of the verse" (Rodgers, "Unleashed").

Melissa with one of her trade-
mark 12-string Ovation guitars

Essentially, though, the entire album is a brilliant, searing cry of the heart. It's an articulate turmoil of jealousy, passion, and unrequited love spanning several shattered relationships. Even the ballads, such as "Precious Pain," ache and yearn — or, as does "Watching You," they obsess. It struck a resounding emotional chord in one critic, who wrote: "If you have ever lain alone chewing the pillow knowing your lover is enjoying steaming passion in another bed, you'll understand the rampant insanity of 'Bring Me Some Water.' If you've spent day after day and week after week mourning the loss of somebody who you know is never going to come back, you'll understand 'Occasionally.' If you've ever taunted a lover by reminding them of sexual intimacies and inadequacies they'd really rather forget, then you'll understand the new single, 'Similar Features' " (Kirk).

Other cuts on the album include "Chrome Plated Heart," "Don't You Need," "The Late September Dogs" (which several critics have claimed sounds like something Springsteen might have put on *Nebraska*), and "I Want You." Etheridge has this to say about the album's content: "I just tried to put together my best, most passionate songs, and it turned out that my conflicts with jealousy and pain are the most powerful emotions" (qtd. in Segell). Despite these harrowing flash points, though, the album is also about strength: having it and finding it. "I take pride in considering myself a strong woman out there fighting for my career and relationships," states Melissa. "I write best when it comes from something I know and feel, something that affects me, something that I learned or that I can't get through. Whatever it is, I'm not afraid to put it down honestly" (qtd. in Mason).

Island did not actually release *Melissa Etheridge* until 2 May 1988, although the disk had been recorded and mixed in 1987. Chris Blackwell decided to introduce Melissa in

England, and so she crossed the pond and spent April and May of 1988 on tour. The idea was to have Etheridge gain a certain popular momentum abroad before she tackled her home turf. Consequently, it was in England that Melissa first heard herself on the radio. She described how it happened during her 1994 VH-1 Roots of Rock and Roll concert: driving down a street, she heard a familiar riff on the radio and thought, "Oh, I know this song"; in a flash, she realized that it was "Similar Features." Elsewhere she adds, "I sat there and cried. . . . It was an incredible experience" (qtd. in "Rocker").

Melissa opened for a band called Martin Stephenson and the Dainties. They covered the territory exhaustively, small English towns and large centers alike. In general, Melissa was well received, but the fact that she played a twelve-string acoustic guitar was a source of confusion for many. It led them to assume that she was folk-oriented, but then, hearing her rock, they didn't know how to categorize her. *Melody Maker* critic Paul Mathur, writing in June of 1988, seemed a bit bewildered and (for no obvious reason) angry: "At a showcase gig in London," Etheridge "impressed hardened hacks and cynical drunks (or is it the other way round?) with her raw-edged lyricism, her apparent belief that sometimes things turn out right, but most of the time they don't. And, yes, yes, yes, she's another bloody singer-songwriter."

This critic was speaking for a segment of the listening public that believes many singer-songwriters exploit personal suffering — to banal effect — with the idea that they are creating powerful art. Etheridge found it baffling that by merely being a singer-songwriter she could incite debate over the issue of musical authenticity. It became apparent that her career was not going to take off in England. Strangely, it never has. As recently as 1996, Melissa told Rockline that she could count on always being able to vacation in peace, without being recognized, in at least one English-speaking country.

England's reluctance to embrace Etheridge may simply be due to stereotypical British reserve, to that native automatic recoil from emotional display. Still, Etheridge managed to penetrate some defences. Mathur did venture to comment, "She's not there yet, but the promise is tantilisingly great." Kris Kirk, who reviewed her debut album for *Melody Maker* in May of 1988, had a slightly more favorable impression. Admitting that the album had not been easy for him to listen to, he concluded: "Raw is the key word, and this is the rawest of albums. As in callow. And as in cold, bleak, rawness of emotion. Somewhere along the line this woman has been emotionally skinned alive and it's precisely because she's such a mass of exposed nerves and bare bones that to admit deriving pleasure from her album is to virtually confess one is a sadist." But he also called the album "brave," and added that he was "dying to see what she does next."

When *Melissa Etheridge* hit the United States, the reviews were more positive. Etheridge's showcase performances at the Roxy in Los Angeles and at New York's Beacon Theater were critical successes. But Etheridge ran into the problem of categorization stateside as well. After longtime Etheridge fan Bonnie Vader saw Melissa perform at a Greenwich Village bar called Crazy Nanny's in 1989, she went out hunting for a tape of the debut album because she just had to have "Like the Way I Do." In a Brooklyn record store, she asked a sales clerk about the song. "Yes, I believe it's on the same tape as 'Bring Me Some Water,'" he responded, and then directed Bonnie to the country-music section.

Scrambling to quantify what they were seeing and hearing by likening Etheridge to known entities, American reviewers evoked the names of Janis Joplin, Bonnie Raitt,

Bonnie Tyler, and Kim Carnes. The pronouncement that she was a female Springsteen rapidly became a cliché. Was Etheridge a kind of yuppie Joplin? Reacting to this rude charge, one writer snapped, "she's too rough-edged to be a yuppie. John Hiatt and Chrissie Hynde are more her style" (Tough). Etheridge claims she even read one review that described her as "Joni Mitchell-meets-John Cougar Mellencamp" (qtd. in "Rocker"). A few reviewers actually dared to compare her to sixties belter Melanie. The oddest, though maybe the most flattering, comparison was this: "Etheridge's gritty blues delivery more closely recalls such singers as Etta James and Esther Phillips" (Tomlinson).

Most new sensations fall victim to the facile categorizers, but the fact that Melissa got more than her share may simply be attributable to bad timing. The year of her debut, 1988, was the music industry's famous Year of the Woman. A bumper crop of female singer-songwriters was busy making its mark: Tracy Chapman and Edie Brickell released their debut albums; Suzanne Vega, Michelle Shocked, Toni Childs, and Sinéad O'Connor were hailed for their work, as well. Journalists were forever cramming them together and building single review articles around them, devoting only two or three paragraphs to each. Such tactics were bound to create mix-ups. Etheridge remarks: "I remember when my album came out it was the year that Tracy Chapman and Michelle Shocked and Edie Brickell and all these artists came out, and they kept lumping us together. They'd do these reviews and there would be seven pictures. And I just kind of got that folk image hung around my neck" ("Kansas Girl").

Still, Etheridge was beginning to stockpile some glowing assessments. The *New York Daily News* said, "this debut album may serve to introduce Melissa Etheridge as one of the first rock singers to articulate the complex relationship between melody and rhythm" (Wyatt). *People* assured its readers that Etheridge definitely "deserves some checking out," and that together Etheridge, Krampf, and McCormick "muster a bigger, deeper sound than their numbers might indicate" (Novak, "Melissa Etheridge"). The album sold slowly, however, and the big music publications such as *Rolling Stone* didn't even bother to review it.

There were also, inevitably, a few negative reviews of *Melissa Etheridge*. When she opened in October of 1988 for Bruce Hornsby and the Range at the renowned Beacon Theater, *Billboard* grumbled, "Opener Melissa Etheridge wallowed deeply in moaning self-pity during heart-break songs from her eponymous Island Records debut" ("Talent in Action"). A *Savvy Woman* reviewer cautioned: "Although Etheridge is an inventive musician, her lyrics are largely restricted to variations on the theme of obsessive romance. She's what self-help pundits like to call a Woman Who Loves Too Much." While "There's nothing wrong with singing the blues, of course," and Etheridge's performances "are often haunting . . . she's not yet a songwriter capable of stretching one bad affair into an entire album" (Tough).

In pieces such as these, there was such tangible discomfort at the in-your-face quality of her emotional expression that Etheridge felt compelled to protest that she was *not* the jilted, tormented soul reviewers were making her out to be. Prior to a five-day engagement at the Roxy in October of 1989, Melissa told the *L.A. Times*, "I don't like the fact that people think I'm this depressed, miserable person. . . . Some people come to see me wallow in misery. Men write me letters telling me how they want to help me become a happy person." She then added, "I'm sensitive to pain — to other people's pain. That doesn't mean I've experienced all the pain I write about. Let's say I have a good imagination. . . . If I was like the characters in some of my songs, I probably would have committed suicide years ago" (qtd. in Hunt). Later, Etheridge quoted B.B. King on playing the blues to one of her concert audiences: "People who sing the blues don't really have the blues, because they sing about it." Then she quipped: "You should try it." Clearly, Etheridge's songwriting is grounded in personal experience, but intensified through the filter of her imagination to achieve the lyrical and musical effects she's looking for.

Longtime fan John Miller remembers seeing a particularly passionate performance Etheridge gave at Slim's in San Francisco in October of 1988. Since late summer, the Bay Area's radio station KOFY had been spinning "Bring Me Some Water" relentlessly, and John, for one, was primed for Melissa's arrival. "This was the most dynamic performer I had heard in years," he says. He'd bought the cassette of her debut album and had listened to it over and over again. "Struck by the intensity of her clenched-fist image on the cover," he recalls, "I frequently found myself staring" at it. Nothing could induce him to miss her San Francisco appearance.

Slim's was a new club, owned by seventies crooner Boz Scaggs. Shortly after the doors opened, John showed up expecting to secure a spot for himself near the stage; after all, Etheridge was relatively unknown (even John's DJ friends had been unable to serve him up any information about her), and it was a Wednesday night. But there "already was a huge crowd of women crushed against the stage," and John realized that he'd probably get no closer than fifteen to twenty feet from the star attraction. Claiming the best position he could find, he settled in to wait for showtime. He then found he couldn't help eavesdropping on — and gradually joining in — the conversations going on around him. A lot of the assembled women went way back with Melissa. They had journeyed up, that day, from their home territory of southern California where they had often gone to see Melissa when she was playing the women's bar and the festival circuits. A large contingent of her old groupies was there, intent on the project of following Melissa around on her first tour. Some of the women John spoke to told him they "viewed their support of Melissa as a political act." The line he kept hearing from these women was that their purpose was "helping to increase dyke visibility."

All this came as a huge revelation to John: he hadn't known his new musical heroine was gay. Suddenly he saw that the lyrical power of this music that had had such a profound physical and emotional impact on him emanated from its creator's desire for *women*. Instead of feeling excluded and turning away, John became even more intrigued. "Though I had been listening to so-called 'women's music' for years," he reflects, "I had seldom heard lyrics so raw, so passionate." The effect was thoroughly "refreshing." Finally, he thought, somebody had burst upon the scene with the courage to "challeng[e] the narrow attitudes which had kept 'women's music' off mainstream labels for so long."

When Melissa finally took over Slim's stage, John says, she performed "well beyond my [already elevated] expectations." She "owned the stage that night. . . . [A]ll of us who were seeing her for the first time were amazed at her power, her control, her charisma, and her rapport with the audience." After more than thirty years of concert-going (Hendrix, Joplin, Cream, and the Jefferson Airplane number among the highlights), John is still able to declare that seeing Melissa Etheridge perform live was "the most intense music experience of my life."

Melissa was keeping busy. She spent a good half year touring small venues; she did a few dates in Europe towards the end of 1988, opening for Huey Lewis and the

News; and she made the rounds of the radio stations, playing for live broadcast. On the heels of this period of hard labor came two big breaks. Melissa was more than ready for them. The first was an invitation to appear on *Late Night with David Letterman* on 13 December 1988. Her hair spiked, tricked out in black pants, a bolo tie, dangling earrings, a bracelet, and a jacket with rolled-up sleeves, Melissa covered "Bring Me Some Water" with Letterman's house band. Bandleader Paul Shaffer danced and clapped his hands in the background. At the end of the show, there was one minor glitch: Letterman turned to Melissa and said, "Have a great holiday, Susan." Nonplussed, Melissa still rallied and did the politically astute thing — she sent champagne over to Letterman's staff as an expression of thanks for their role in assuring her

*Melissa
sporting a
spiky 'do*
FOTEX / SHOOTING STAR

appearance went smoothly. Letterman was, after all, a powerful friend to have.

The Letterman performance brought Etheridge excellent national exposure and opened the door for her to become a show favorite. She was asked back several months later, in March, to do "Similar Features." This time, she wore a tie-dyed T-shirt and a black vest, and had Shaffer accompany her on keyboards. Proof positive that Melissa had truly earned Letterman's admiration had already come in the form of an invitation to participate in his anniversary show, which aired in early February 1989. Melissa relates the experience: "I remember standing one foot away from Al Green in the rehearsal room and going 'A-a-a-ah' — my knees went out. . . . I hadn't sung backup since high school, and they said, 'Here, you take the low part.' The whole thing was pretty exciting; Carlos Santana was playing in the band, and here I was backing up Al Green and Tom Jones" (qtd. in Tomlinson). That trio of Letterman appearances attracted some important attention. Arsenio Hall booked Melissa, and on his high-profile late-night groove-fest she covered "Bring Me Some Water" and "Chrome Plated Heart." On MTV's *Mouth-to-Mouth*, she did a rousing rendition of "Like the Way I Do."

A midnight call from manager Bill Leopold brought Etheridge news of the second big break. "Bring Me Some Water" had been nominated for a Grammy. Island's promotional efforts — for example, the glossy printed material and the promo CD with the live tracks — had been well aimed and had hit their mark. The company's Boston strategy was typical of their overall marketing plan: there Island had treated area radio, press, and retail people to a private harbor cruise that included a live, on-board Etheridge performance.

Recovering from her initial shock, Melissa commented: "I feel like I've got a one-in-four chance" to win the award.

The other nominees are "all great performers, and I'm excited and honored to be in that category" (qtd. in Mohn). The category she was referring to was a newly created one: Best Female Rock Vocal Performance. Etheridge found herself pitted against the likes of Tina Turner, Toni Childs, and Sinéad O'Connor. But then a great thing got even better. Etheridge was asked to perform her celebrated song on the live television broadcast of the Grammy Awards ceremony, along with the other women in her category.

On the big night, Melissa was thrilled to find herself seated behind Joni Mitchell. But, as she told VH-I's *Two Dollar Stare* later that year, she was also "scared to death." Before performing, Melissa and her band had to stand in place behind a lowered curtain for about three minutes. "My life passed before my eyes." To a Canadian music-video channel, Musique Plus, she also admitted that she'd had a terrible case of dry mouth. In front of the curtain, emcee Billy Crystal was introducing Etheridge by quipping, "Born and raised in Kansas, she got her first guitar at eight, started writing songs at ten, and had a record at 11:30, I think." The audience, packed with music-industry heavyweights and glitterati, was still laughing as the curtain went up. Melissa moved rapidly forward, strumming her Ovation, and came to a halt before the microphone, bathed in a spotlight. "Thank you," she said, and stepped away. Light flooded the stage, revealing the band behind her; they launched into "Bring Me Some Water," which took exactly 240 adrenalin-charged seconds to perform. Melissa played and sang flawlessly, often growling the lyrics into the mike, and on that night — 22 February 1989 — won a whole new following. Tina Turner claimed the award, but Etheridge was flying high. The next week, *Melissa Etheridge* jumped sixteen spots up the Billboard charts. A few weeks later, the album finally went gold in the United States, peaking at number 22 on 13 May. In Canada and Australia, where Etheridge's talent had been recognized much more rapidly, the rewards were even greater: *Melissa Etheridge* went platinum in Canada and double platinum in Australia.

Yet by the time Melissa was finally being lauded for her first album, she had already embarked on her next. In January of 1989, she put in three days of studio time recording tracks for *Brave and Crazy*. May of that year would see her spend another three days in studio. Album number two was released on 11 September 1989. Profiting from the experience she had gained the first time around, Etheridge acted as her own producer in conjunction with bassist Kevin McCormick and engineer Niko Bolas. Again, Waddy Wachtel did some guitar overdubbing, and Scott Thurston did the same on keyboards. The band had had some trouble recruiting a steady guitarist, but by now this particular wrinkle had been ironed out: Bernie Larsen was filling the bill and doing keyboards too. Reviewers were quick to note that *Brave and Crazy* had come out suspiciously soon after the debut album, but most were not aware that *Melissa Etheridge* had been recorded in 1987, not 1988, the year of its release. During the actual two-year interval between the albums, Etheridge had penned plenty of new material. Furthermore, some of the songs on *Brave and Crazy* predated the recording of the first album; Melissa had even had the opportunity to try some of the new songs out on her audiences, most notably those she serenaded during a short summer tour she did as opening act for Little Feat.

Etheridge has described the *Brave and Crazy* songs as "a little more extroverted, less into dark corners. . . . [But] I wouldn't call them happy" (qtd. in Outerbridge). On Rockline in 1993, Melissa said simply that the first album had been a learning experience, and that the kind of material it contained was much the same as *Brave and Crazy*'s. By the time her second album was in production, however, she felt she had learned how to play better with her band.

Brave and Crazy took off. It went gold two short weeks after its release. Still, a lot of critics have pronounced it Etheridge's worst effort: as recently as 1996, Britain's *Q* magazine allotted it only one star, and described it as a "weedy set of songs that even Bonnie Raitt would have rejected for being too old hat" (Aizlewood); *Rolling Stone* didn't even deign to review it; *Stereo Review* said, "Taken in small doses, Etheridge is quite effective. Over the course of an entire album, however, the repetitiveness and narrowness of her music get a little tiresome" (Givens). Even Chris Blackwell had ambivalent feelings about the album. *Brave and Crazy* "wasn't bad, but it wasn't great. I wasn't particularly keen on it, but [Melissa] liked it and I supported it" (qtd. in Everett).

Despite its lackluster reception in certain quarters, though, the album garnered another Grammy nomination for Etheridge. After all, it does boast what Etheridge fans are fond of referring to as the greatest line-up of tracks on any album, ever: "You Used to Love to Dance" followed by "The Angels" followed by "You Can Sleep while I Drive" followed by "Testify." And some critics did respond more positively to *Brave and Crazy* than to *Melissa Etheridge* because a little humor had worked its way into the chronicles of pain and despair it contains. Melissa had learned to be a bit more subtle. *Guitar Player* magazine elaborates: "Pushed along by some fine fretted and fretless bass work by bandmember/co-producer Kevin McCormick, Etheridge's songs carry their characteristic preoccupations with emotional estrangement and lusty idealism, but frame them in a more refined, funky, and bluesy package than last year's debut" (Resnicoff). A *New*

York magazine reviewer had this to say: "I was expecting [Etheridge's] newest album . . . to suffer from the usual sophomore slump. But it doesn't. In a bold departure from her debut, not all of the album's songs are about love and lust. 'You Can Sleep while I Drive' . . . is a feminine version of Bruce Springsteen's 'Born to Run,' a nice touch considering that Etheridge's wiry intensity has often been compared to that of the Boss himself" (Wurtzel). "In terms of musicianship alone," *People* magazine concluded, "Etheridge certainly proves herewith that she belongs among the major figures of the record business — her talents and tastes may well help define the music of her generation" (Novak, "Brave and Crazy").

Although both albums consist of ten tracks of original music, ten odes to failed relationships, *Brave and Crazy* is not quite as raw as the debut disk. *Brave and Crazy's* first single, "No Souvenirs," is a lament for the loss of a loved one and a promise to remain, despite the rupture, that lover's emotional mainstay. But the lover has moved beyond reach — she's selling her car; her mail has been forwarded — and she has left behind no souvenirs. The video of this song is striking: it opens with Etheridge sitting on the edge of what appears to be a rooftop, her legs dangling over the side and her booted feet planted in a rowboat. It is essentially a performance video, but there are quick cuts to images of Etheridge burning a letter or slicing a piece of fruit.

The first verse of "No Souvenirs" contains some lines that fans have fretted over for years. Etheridge makes a call from "a jackpot telephone," and sings of how she loves her lover's name and the way her lover makes "the buffalo roam." During a 1989 concert at New York City's Bottom Line, Etheridge clarified things a bit. She introduced the song by saying: "This next song I like to call my song about modern romance. It's all about I've got a job, I've got a career — they're not jobs anymore; they're careers — you've got a career, you've got a phone machine, I've got a phone machine. I'll call your phone machine and I'll meet you sometime next month about Thursday at four o'clock." "You know," she continued, "it's all about trying to fit love and romance in between all that stuff, and it gets hard, and this song is a result of that. I learned if you don't take care of things, if you don't get priorities straight . . . things kind of fade away, and hearts get broken."

The point of "No Souvenirs," concluded one reviewer, "seems to be that life has gotten so impersonal, so technological, that we can't even talk to each other face-to-face anymore" (Wurtzel). Etheridge has also spoken about the song in more direct and personal terms: ". . . I was having sort of a long distance relationship, an affair — it was not even a relationship, it was merely an affair — and I remembered making a phone call on a pay-phone machine, and it reminded me of slipping the money in." The purpose of the call was to decide, once and for all, whether the affair would "go on" or "be over. And it was like gambling to me, it was like I was putting in my money and I was going to pull the handle and it was either going to come up or it wasn't. To me it was like a jackpot, a one armed bandit, a slot machine" ("The Only One").

As for the roaming buffalo, one rumor that circulated among Etheridge fans for a long time is that it is an oblique reference to a buffalo pendant one of her former lovers used to wear. The pendant would "roam" all over Melissa's body as her partner hovered over her during lovemaking. Melissa finally confirmed the story while taping an episode of VH-1's *Storytellers*, which aired in November of 1996.

"No Souvenirs" just seems to go on generating insights into Melissa's emotional landscape. A *Spin* reporter remarked that the songs on *Brave and Crazy* "aren't as overtly concerned with relationships as the ones on

Melissa Etheridge." She then added, " 'No Souvenirs' is very descriptive, more about the world outside of yourself." Melissa answered her like this: "I've grown a little in the field of relationships — just a little bit. I think I have more control on jealousy [laughs]. Instead of putting it all on the other person, I'm seeing if I can make myself happy, since I can't depend on *you* to. I'm letting go of a few things and taking care of the inside." "No Souvenirs," she explains, "was a relationship that was purely external. The person was there and then they were gone and nothing was changed, nothing reminded me of them. Nothing. You didn't leave your shoes, you didn't leave this or that. It was very quick" (qtd. in Schoemer).

The demise of a romantic union is also the focus of "You Used to Love to Dance" and of "You Can Sleep while I Drive." In the former, which in concert Melissa has described as a song about "the one that got away," the singer's lover has departed because she wasn't getting what she needed and wanted to return to the concrete- and-steel core of the city. The abandoned partner remi- nisces longingly about laughing and drinking on Saturday nights in a "downtown dive," where the cover charge was only fifty cents and every love song was theirs alone.

"You Can Sleep while I Drive" — which Etheridge has performed as a duet with both k.d. lang and Jewel, and which country-music star Trisha Yearwood covered in 1995 — is a lover's plea to her partner to come with her as she leaves town in search of a better life. They'll travel through Tucson, Santa Fe, Nashville, and New Orleans. (The "Bar- bara in Nashville" mentioned in this song is, incidentally, a real person: Barb Savage, who, along with Melissa's ex-lover Kathleen Mahoney, is a past producer of Rhythm- fest, a woman's music festival traditionally held near Atlanta over the Labor Day weekend). The wistful quality of the lyrics and the tenor of the song suggest, though, that the singer knows she has already lost. Her lover cannot be persuaded to make a leap of faith.

Brave and Crazy's third single (the second single released was "Let Me Go") is called "The Angels." It's a catchy tune that Melissa says heralds a shift in her attitude towards her old fixations: "Last year I let go of a lot of things. That's what 'The Angels' is. It's the same relationship as 'Bring Me Some Water,' same relationship as 'Like the Way I Do,' but I said, I'm just going to let go of this or I'm going to go out of my mind. 'All I want is for your love to be all mine, but the angels won't have it.' So there. I've definitely changed about love and romance. I've lost a lot of the initial, 'God, I'm in love and this is forever' kind of thing. 'Cause you know that it's *not* forever" (qtd. in Schoemer).

The "Angels" video has a special significance. It was directed by Julie Cypher, with whom Melissa eventually fell in love (ironically, the " 'forever' kind of thing"), and stars Lou Diamond Phillips, who was Cypher's husband at the time. Melissa plays the part of a single mom with a young daughter — she even wears a housedress! — and Phillips is an angel who observes their daily routine. Before long, it becomes clear that the angel is in love with the young mother; in one scene, Melissa sleeps as Phillips tenderly strokes her cheek. Phillips falls from the sky, his wings vanish, and he becomes human. The little girl rushes over to where he lies dazed on the ground. He looks up and there is Melissa, smiling down at him. The video ends with the three of them walking away together.

Etheridge claims that another standout track on *Brave and Crazy*, "Testify," is actually not a love song at all. Rather, as she told the crowd during one of her 1989 Bottom Line gigs, it's about how easy it is, in this day and age, to just tune things out. "You have to let yourself feel," she urged. Some have insisted that the song was written with slain San Francisco gay activist Harvey Milk in mind; Melissa was inspired by a film about Milk called *The Mayor of Castro Street*.

Among the more playful cuts on the album are the funky "Brave and Crazy," "Let Me Go," and "Skin Deep." Etheridge has explained how the title track took shape. "A lot of these tunes grew on the road," she says. "I wrote 'Brave and Crazy' mainly as just a guitar song — that G chord with a c# added is actually a mistake I played when I went to hit a G7. Then I started doing it with Kevin and Fritz, and over about a year, it developed. I really liked what Kevin started doing on it, and encouraged him to 'Do more of that, do more of that,' and it just became a really strong bass-riff song" (qtd. in Resnicoff).

The remaining *Brave and Crazy* tracks include "My Back Door," which revolves around the loss of illusions and the loss of passion and the struggle to regain them, and "Royal Station 4/16." The latter is Melissa's "train song," written on 16 April 1988, during her promotional tour of England, at a hotel called the Royal Station. U2-heads gravitate to this cut because Bono helped it along by playing the harmonica. He just happened to be at the A & M studios while Melissa was recording *Brave and Crazy*, and wandered in to listen to her perform. On impulse, Melissa invited him to join in. Bono listened to "Royal Station 4/16" a few times and then pulled off the harmonica solo.

Reviews of the album had been mixed, and so were the concert reviews throughout the *Brave and Crazy* tour. In the course of a minitour that was scheduled for the month of the album's release, Etheridge made her second appearance at the Bottom Line; she played five nights at that famous venue, along with the Subdudes (she also did similar extended engagements in Chicago, Toronto, and Los Angeles). It is as if the reviewers of these shows had not been to see the same performer. The *New York Daily*

Melissa at work

News, under the headline "Melissa Etheridge Does a Phony Joni," fumed, "As she proved repeatedly during her first five nights at the club, the excessively perky Etheridge exhibits an overbearing phoniness that belies her Earth-mama image." As his attack gained momentum, the reviewer threw in: "Watch Melissa shake her mane and grimace during the 'rockers.' Watch Melissa close her eyes and glance upward during the 'sensitive' ballads. Watch Melissa run to each side of the tiny Bottom Line stage to encourage more people to applaud. What initially seemed like fiery spunk deteriorated to mannered posing." He referred to Etheridge's cover of Marvin Gaye's "Let's Get It On" as a "screech-fest," and ended the review by announcing that " 'Skin Deep' . . . summed up her performance and her music all too well" (Browne).

Yet in its review of the same set of performances, *Billboard* enthused: "By the time [Etheridge] wrapped up with a triple-play of 'Bring Me Some Water' and 'Like the Way I Do,' linked by Marvin Gaye's 'Let's Get It On,' she had whipped her fans into a near-frenzied state. And if some of the moves seemed straight out of Rock 'N' Roll Guitar Playing 101, they were unfailingly convincing and unpretentious" (Newman, "Talent in Action"). The *New York Tribune* hailed the performances; the Bottom Line was emphatically not the scene of a poseur's screech-fest, but of a rapturous celebration: "The room was full, a standing-room line that had snaked up the block was now packed together at the bar, and from the moment Etheridge hit the stage she was greeted with an explosive response. Finally . . . Melissa Etheridge was getting the kind of attention that her music seems to demand." The *Trib* marveled at the "difference a year makes," pointing out that Etheridge's last New York gig had been warming up for Bruce Hornsby and the Range at the Beacon — a performance that lasted all of thirty-five minutes (Ruhlmann).

Karen Leo, a veteran Etheridge supporter, saw four of the five Bottom Line shows. Each was as great as the next, she says, but one stands out in her mind. On that night, Karen recalls, Melissa was performing "You Can Sleep while I Drive," and right after the bridge, when she sang "lover you're free / Can't you get that with me?" there was an instant of total silence. Someone in the audience interjected, very softly, "Yes." "Melissa cracked up," says Karen. "It took her a few seconds to get it together again."

Etheridge was still able to hang out with her fans for awhile after her shows — signing autographs and posing for snapshots — without getting mobbed. Karen, a guitarist herself, caught up with Kevin, Fritz, and Melissa out on the sidewalk after one Bottom Line performance and chatted with Melissa about her Adamas. Karen asked Melissa what her equalizer setting was. As she responded, Kevin broke in, saying, "Yeah, and we turn the flanger all the way up" — referring to an effect that Melissa would never use in her music. Melissa turned and looked at Kevin as if he had lost his mind. But then Kevin smiled, and soon they all began to laugh uproariously.

But those days of mingling with the crowd, not a bodyguard in sight, were on the wane. Etheridge's career had reached a crossroads, and now it would either languish or soar.

"Lifebeat" benefit concert
Beacon Theater, NYC
June 24, 1994

Maple Leaf Gardens
Toronto, Canada
March 18, 1996

"VH-1 Duets"
Doheny Mansion, L.A.
October 10, 1995

Melissa and Julie Cypher

"Yes I Am" tour
Summer 1995

Hard Rock Hotel
May 18, 1995

Melissa and John Shanks

Melissa and Dave Beyer

West Coast Women's Music and Comedy Festival
Santa Barbara, CA 1983

Melissa and Julie Cypher

Melissa at age 20
Christmas 1981

Melissa relaxes after a Youth
Group retreat in 1979

Five

NO FEAR

Canadians are no fools. At the 1990 Juno Awards (Canada's Grammy equivalent), Melissa Etheridge was named Best International Artist, a distinction that had at that point only been granted to two other acts: U2 and the Rolling Stones. Canada loved Melissa from the outset. Her first arena-sized venue had been the Montreal Forum; in 1996 she was honored by being selected as the last performer to appear at that hallowed institution (the Beatles were the first, in 1964) before it closed up shop and relocated to shiny new premises.

It all began when her debut album was released, and Melissa demonstrated her willingness to travel to local radio stations where she would play live. This is how Melissa took Canada, helped along by the live promo CD that Island issued in December of 1988. The disk included the live version of "Like the Way I Do," and, says local Etheridge enthusiast David Johnson, that anthem numbered among the top ten most requested radio hits in Montreal for over four months. Melissa's debut album was a top-twenty bestseller in Canada for an entire year.

What finally knocked it off the charts? *Brave and Crazy*, its successor.

German audiences had also fallen for Melissa well in advance of their American counterparts. And one of Melissa's most precious concert memories is of Berlin: she was there, by chance, when the Wall came down in 1989. Steve Folsom, Melissa's sound engineer, remarks that "many things . . . have happened [to us when touring], but the Berlin Wall was the biggest. We all climbed up on top, like the cover of Life Magazine." "We were hearing on the radio that things [in Berlin] were happening; things were very electrified," says Melissa. "At that point, people were leaving East Germany and traveling all the way through Hungary and Austria and coming up around and going back. . . . [W]e didn't know whether we should go to Berlin — maybe there would be trouble, you know?" ("Yes, She Is"). But Etheridge's tour manager, Uli Peretz, who was German, urged them to push on; if they ran into any trouble, he said, they'd still be able to turn back.

They arrived in Berlin the morning of the Wall's timely demise. Melissa woke up on the bus to find they were trapped within the massive traffic jam that occurred as soon as the portals were opened and East Germans began pouring into West Germany. The next day, a free concert was held at a stadium by the Wall. "There were a lot of German acts, and Joe Cocker, and us, in this show," Melissa remembers. "Everybody came to that, and you could tell the East Germans from the West Germans because the East Germans were standing there with their mouths open . . . they'd not seen a rock concert before." Her concert that night was "a big . . . well, it was like a party, but not a drunk, weird party. It was like everyone was just high. It was an amazing part of history, and we were there and high on freedom. Very, very inspiring. Very hopeful" ("Yes, She Is").

The *Brave and Crazy* tour finally wound down. By then, Melissa had toured steadily for two and a half years, and was in dire need of a break. She didn't tour at all in 1991, opting instead to focus her attention on personal things (about which she would later speak publicly) and to record — slowly and painstakingly this time — her next album, *Never Enough*. The fans who had so eagerly embraced *Melissa Etheridge* and *Brave and Crazy* were starved for her next offering by the time of its release date — 9 March 1992. The aptly titled *Never Enough* began to fly off record store shelves. But who was that seductive creature adorning the cover? Not the dark-haired, feisty Melissa of the first two albums. Here was a woman with long, blonde hair; she was shirtless, her bare back turned to the camera, a hint of right breast showing, a Silvertone guitar with its unmistakably feminine curves parked against her hip. (The pose recalls Springsteen's on the cover of *Born in the U.S.A.*) Inside the lyrics booklet of the CD are more photographic portraits of a transformed Etheridge: in one she wears full makeup; in another she's attired in a frilly white blouse and looks an awful lot like country sweetheart Tanya Tucker.

Some fans of long standing instantly disliked the album, insisting that Melissa had sold out to "*Mister* Record Company" — she'd softened her true image into a stereotype of femininity just to expand both audience and profits. A cover controversy ensued, sparking so much debate that virtually every record and concert review published over the course of the next year made mention of it. When Melissa paid a visit to his show again in June of 1992, David Letterman even asked her if she'd felt uncomfortable posing for the cover photo. Jay Leno on the *Tonight Show* cracked a joke about wanting to see the same pose shot from the other side. Some reviewers were actually still commenting on the cover two years later in their assessments of Etheridge's *next* album. Spin controllers at Island had to coax Wal-Mart and K-Mart to display the album; the megachains had shown signs of balking when confronted with that glimpse of Melissa's breast.

Never Enough was also an affront to some of Etheridge's faithful followers because it represents a musical and lyrical departure from the first two albums. For one thing, it features a song called "The Boy Feels Strange," a ballad about wanting to reach out and help a "boy" who is acting strangely, as though he is in a lot of pain. Melissa had always sung gender-neutral songs. She had always spoken to *"you,"* not "he" or "she." Those who knew Etheridge was a lesbian believed "The Boy Feels Strange" to be a blatant lie — the story of a homosexual relationship distorted to create a tale of conventional heterosexuality in order to appease mainstream listeners. Much later on, Etheridge joked that even Kevin McCormick, after first hearing the song, asked her if she'd been up to something he didn't know about.

Not as much of a rocker as its two predecessors, *Never Enough* even boasts a piano ballad called "The Letting Go." Then there's "Place Your Hand," on which young actor Dermot Mulroney plays cello. A dance song rounds things out: called "2001," the tune is driven by a funky, industrial percussion beat. It sounds a lot like a James Brown number. This was not the Melissa Etheridge they knew and loved, and a significant portion of her fans were not pleased.

The critics, however, were another story. They loved *Never Enough*, and seemed, in general, to appreciate its creator's intentions. "I wanted to go in a new direction," Melissa explained to Musique Plus. She *wanted* to make a studio album — overdubs, sampling, and all. She *wanted* to inject dance rhythms into her music because she'd absorbed such rhythms — working it out to the Brothers

Johnson, the Ohio Players, and Earth, Wind and Fire — as a kid thirsty for new sounds. Rock and roll had not been

her be all and end all. She *wanted* to stretch a little and play some piano. In the Netherlands, where fans were still happily reeling from her Pink Pop Festival appearance in June of 1990, Melissa told an interviewer: "I've learned to sing another way. Before, I used to throw myself completely into one song. I gave everything I had in *one* song. Now I've divided this energy over the whole album." *Never Enough* was also intended to be a "thinking" album and a respite from the darkness that seemed to pervade her previous efforts: "The first two albums are very dark. I did make an effort on this album to include more of the lighter side of myself" (qtd. in Rotenstein).

The care, the reflection, and the hard work Melissa poured into *Never Enough* are manifested by the fact that she recorded twenty-three songs for it — songs that span a range of styles. "I picked the ones that came to the top," she says (qtd. in Saxberg). The choices truly were hers: Melissa and Kevin McCormick produced this album alone. Melissa knew her own mind, and had come to trust Kevin's input implicitly. As she told Musique Plus, "I know [Kevin's] music, and I know his talent. And I know that when I ask him, 'do you think this sounds right,' 'do you think this is good,' and he says, 'yes,' then I know he's being truthful." Elsewhere, she explained the foundations of this trust more explicitly: "Kevin understands like no one else which feelings I want to put into my songs. He's the only one I can trust 100% in that aspect. I don't need to explain anything to him at all. On the contrary, I ask for his advice if I doubt whether a song is good or not." Just like she does herself, "Kevin has the feeling that he's been through an important phase of growth. We have matured, [and] become adults also as creative partners" (qtd. in Rotenstein).

About the cover photo: it was not the brainchild of a greedy record company that has no qualms about exploiting its artists in order to boost sales. It was all Melissa's idea. As the final photo session for the album was drawing to a close, she found herself dissatisfied with what they had produced. She'd been struggling to come up with a cover image that was powerful enough — and yet subtle enough — to embody the album's content: something raw, sensual, feminine, and strong. The photo team rolled up their sleeves and went back to work, this time developing an image that fulfilled Etheridge's requirements, but left her open to the charge that she'd bought in to the beauty myth. "I don't think that being pretty means you're not strong or you can only be pretty for men," she later replied. "I was being pretty for my lover" (qtd. in Phoenix). Strangely, "Mister Record Company" himself, Chris Blackwell, hated the cover of *Never Enough*. He didn't even particularly like the album, calling it "flat" (qtd. in Everett).

To a Canadian television interviewer, Etheridge delved even deeper as she tried to justify her choice of cover image to her fans: "I think this 'womanliness' [quoting the interviewer] is something that has been coming about in me and I've been learning about in the last few years. I think I sometimes suppressed it years ago, and have been coming to terms with it and realize that womanliness does not equal weakness. I think that's what I'm really trying to present in this album cover and music." But by the time she spoke to *Rolling Stone* about it in 1994, she was able to joke: "If you would gather up all my videos, you'll see the one thing I never got a handle on was my image. I call myself fashion impaired. So with my third album, I just thought, 'Why do I have to wear clothes at all?'"

The advent of the CD — and the corresponding decline in high-quality album-cover art — was yet another factor

contributing to Etheridge's cover-photo selection. For a
tiny CD cover to command the consumer's attention from
the far side of a vast record store already bursting with
loudly competing images, it has to have ferocious visual
impact. Melissa was well aware of this.

She had known the cover would be talked about. On
Musique Plus and on Rockline, she said she'd even
asked her mom what she thought of the cover shots
before making her final choice. Elizabeth Etheridge
had answered, "Well, Melissa, you're going to have to
answer a lot of questions. And if you can answer the
questions, I see no problem." So at least she had her
mom's permission.

Cover controversy aside, *Never Enough* was busy inspiring critical approval. It even received accolades in some
quarters: *Stereo Review* bestowed its "Heart Attack" performance rating on the album, and called it a "fully-
rounded . . . stunner" (Nash, "Melissa Etheridge"). *People*
pronounced it a "triumph" (Novak, "Never Enough").
On a more cautious note, the *Hollywood Reporter* ventured
to call the album "a welcome return to form after [Ether-
idge's] disappointing *Brave and Crazy*" (Vare). *Guitar Player*
quantified *Never Enough* as "a tantalizing blend of rock,
funk, and folk, with sprinklings of dance and Latin
music," then added, "anyone who's pegged the singer/
guitarist as a sleepy folkie will be rudely awakened by the
aggressive guitar work of Etheridge and session guitarists
Steuart Smith and Mark Goldenberg" (Smith). *CD Review*
had this to say: Etheridge "comes out determined to take
on anyone and anything in 'Ain't It Heavy,' featuring a
big ol' backbeat, a fiery blend of acoustic and electric
guitars, and soul driven chorus. Then we're plunged into
the techno-drenched percussives and surround-sound of
'2001' as Etheridge recounts the betrayals and disappoint-
ments that take down family and friends, one by one. She

then finds a healing balm in the seductively tranquil, yet rhythmic 'Dance Without Sleeping' " (Morden). Much later, *Q* magazine anointed the album with a four-star ranking, proclaimed its production to be "adventurous," and judged its songs "generally better" than those on the earlier albums (Aizlewood).

And *Rolling Stone* could no longer hold itself back. It finally had to review a Melissa Etheridge product. Although "there's nothing as arresting on this album as 'Bring Me Some Water,' " the reviewer remarked, "taken as a whole, *Never Enough* represents Etheridge's best work to date" (Cullen). The *Stone's* audacity was not lost on Melissa, whose first two albums that venerable publication had greeted with icy silence: "They said I had moved to new levels and was solid and proving myself as a writer, but there wasn't anything as classic as 'Bring Me Some Water.' That was funny, because they were calling something classic that they had totally ignored" (qtd. in McTavish).

Never Enough really is an excellent album — if it's taken on its own terms and not as a mere extension of its predecessors. With its techno drums and infectious dance beat, "2001" may well be the track that stands out most forcefully on this album packed with standout tracks. Melissa paved the way for this oddball cut's acceptance by releasing rocker "Ain't It Heavy" as a single first and then following it up with "2001." On one level an exploration of various forces that threaten the planet, "2001" is also a commentary on the impact media images have on our lives. With the millennium approaching, Etheridge anticipates dark years ahead and sings, "Wake me up when we hit 2001."

On Rockline, Melissa explained that the song was more political than anything she'd ever done before. Her main concerns when she penned it were women's rights and the erosion of human rights in general. She plugged the upcoming video of "2001," and, without concealing that she was a strong supporter of presidential candidate Bill Clinton, encouraged the Rockline crowd to get out there and register for the vote. Etheridge had effectively aroused a curiosity in her fans that would not be satisfied. The anticipated premiere of "2001," the video, on MTV never took place. The all-powerful music-video channel sent "2001" back, charging that its representation of the pro-choice/pro-life debate was biased.

Melissa's most complex and ambitious video to date, "2001" was another Julie Cypher production. The clip features an African woman dancing; television images of the Kennedy-Smith rape trial and the Thomas-Hill sexual-harassment hearings; flashed words and phrases, such as "Backlash," "Womyn Reply," and "Hang On." Interspersed with all this are scenes of an older couple — the husband flips through a book of violent pictures — and of a younger couple fighting. The older woman eventually snatches the book from her husband and tosses it away; the younger couple makes up. The words "Ask Why" and "Ask" are then flashed at the viewer: the message is, apparently, that no one has to swallow the status quo whole. Positive change is possible. None of this, however, got under anyone's skin. What unsettled MTV brass was a scene of pro-lifers assembling for a demonstration with the flashing, superimposed message "Protect Choice."

When MTV put down its heavy foot, Julie did some soul-searching. She decided to reedit the video, substituting the words "End Censorship" for "Protect Choice." No dice. MTV people screened the revised clip and passed on it again. It's unclear whether they ever understood that their censorious actions directly mimicked the backlash Etheridge and Cypher were decrying in the video — and clearly demonstrated how pervasive it had become.

Melissa performs "Keep It Precious"
at the March on Washington, 1993
AMY PUTNAM / PEGASUS PHOTOWORKS

"Dance without Sleeping" is another exceptional cut on an album constructed of exceptions. Etheridge explains that its fresh and spontaneous quality is not the result of any technical manipulation. It's real: "Dance without Sleeping" is "a different sort of melody than what I usually do. I asked Kevin and Fritz to come up with a groove, a musical bed with a mid-tempo beat. They brought this tape back to me and I wrote lyrics to it." It wasn't until they were in the studio," she continues, "and the tape was rolling that we cut it. You're hearing the first time I ever sang it. I'm just channelling the melody. It's very special to me, because I'll probably never sing it like that again. It's so tentative and vulnerable because I didn't know what was happening" (qtd. in Trakin). The song's lyrics evoke an atmosphere of resignation. The singer wants to forget everything and dance. She's letting go. She knows that although the stable, protective world she sees portrayed in magazines, on the radio, and on movie screens is power-fully seductive — imagine a place where fathers, mothers, and lovers never leave — it is unattainable. A fairy tale. This woman walks a fine line between anger and under-standing, desperation, and loneliness. She worries about her own capacity for self-deception. As Melissa told Rock-line, this is a complicated song.

Never Enough's last track is called "It's for You." Melissa wrote it for her fans. "I had been off the road for a year and hadn't performed," she recalls, "and I was really, really missing it, and missing the audience and missing just the whole experience of performing for people. And it was like missing a lover. So that's what I wrote about" ("Kan-sas Girl"). Etheridge has always insisted that she writes songs and makes records so that she can perform them. The act of performing gives her a rush that seems beyond the power of words to express. But to a Dutch television audience, she did articulate this much: "The most difficult thing to describe is when I come onstage, and what it's like being onstage. It's a very freeing experience; it's like diving off the highest diving board. It's frightening, but the feeling is so wonderful while you're jumping, and you're hoping the water will be there and that it won't hurt." Playing live, for Etheridge, is "empowering." This moment, no matter how many times she relives it, fills her with awe: she bounds onto the stage and is instantly confronted with a sea of faces; these people from all walks of life, people who encompass insurmountable personal differences, have all converged in this pocket of time and space to share an experience with her.

"It's for You," then, is Etheridge's attempt to give something back to her fans — something that reflects the unique bond between artist and audience. Yet she rarely plays the song in concert, and seems reluctant to explain why. As her *Never Enough* tour was winding down in December of 1992, Melissa did two benefit concerts in Chicago (WXRT's Christmas for Kids). Introducing "It's for You," she teased the audience by saying she never played the song in concert for reasons she wouldn't get into, but she would play it that night. One clue: a fan named Lauren once asked Melissa after a concert in Atlanta why she didn't include the song in her lineup. "It seems like such a natural concert song," Lauren remarked. "*Because* it seems like such a natural concert song," Melissa said, smiling.

While touring to promote the album, Melissa would prime the crowd for another popular track, the love song "Keep It Precious," with the following patter: "There's a secret to love. You gotta work hard at it; you gotta go the ups and downs, the ins and the outs . . . all around, and you've got to keep working at it. You've got to keep it honest, you've gotta keep talking, you've got to keep it . . . precious." In 1993, she disclosed to an interviewer that she had written "Keep It Precious" to break through to a lover when communications between them began to falter:

"We were trying to figure out . . . where we were going, if we were going, where we were going. And this was just my plea, you know, we've gone this far . . . . [and] it's a lot of hard work but let's do it, let's keep it precious, let's work on it, let's hold on, let's hold on to it. It's just a love plea actually" ("The Only One"). That plea has a universal dimension, as well. Because its lyrics are versatile enough to imply even broader kinds of relationships, and because of their inspirational quality, Melissa chose "Keep It Precious" as the song she would perform at the 1993 March on Washington for Lesbian and Gay Rights.

So the romantic rage that had kept *Melissa Etheridge* and *Brave and Crazy* burning at white heat had ebbed by the time *Never Enough* was conceived. Melissa had finally found some peace in her relationships; the old scars were healing. In "Place Your Hand," a song she says is about "the power of intimacy," she wrestles with the demons of failed relationships, then finds that a new romantic union has the power to soothe lingering wounds. The song is about "the vulnerable feelings you have and that momentary release you get when you're physical with another person," explains Melissa (qtd. in Trakin). She likes to perform another *Never Enough* healing song, "The Letting Go," alone at the piano. On these occasions, the old anger is nowhere to be seen or heard: the song is just a mature, heartfelt good-bye.

"Sometimes I know that it's never enough." The first line of the album's preeminent cut, "Ain't It Heavy," encapsulates its title. But *what* is never enough? Etheridge tackles the obvious question by describing a hard-won realization: "I'm not going to find enough in a relationship or in a career or in anything else or anyone else. It's got to come from myself, otherwise it will be never enough"

Melissa with her Grammy award (for "Ain't It Heavy"), 1992

GREG DE GUIRE/
LONDON FEATURES
INT'L USA

(qtd. in Rotenstein). She has also put a more public spin on the song's interpretation: "It's about the survival of a single woman in the '90s. It's about dealing with our sexual lives now in this day of AIDS and sort of trying to find a pleasure that isn't harmful to you or detrimental" (qtd. in Saxberg).

"Ain't It Heavy" scored for Melissa the coup she had been longing for — a major hit of high-profile recognition in the United States. In 1992, she was awarded the Grammy for Best Female Vocal Rock Performance. On a personal level, the honor had a special poignancy. John Etheridge had succumbed to liver cancer in 1991, and Melissa had dedicated *Never Enough* to his memory. His influence is woven through some of the songs on the album. Melissa's friend Mary Chapin Carpenter made the presentation, which took place prior to the awards telecast. Being chosen by her peers above the likes of Lita Ford, Alison Moyet, Alannah Myles, and Tina Turner was potent consolation for the fact that *Never Enough*, despite everything, still had not sold any more copies for Etheridge than her first two albums. (It didn't even go platinum in Australia, where she was used to ruling the charts.) And Melissa was still experiencing some troublesome resistance from radio.

Most album-oriented rock stations were happy to give her a good dose of air time — though some, amazingly, shunned female artists in general, or imposed such zany rules as no more than one woman per hour, or never play two women back-to-back — but Top 40 had no place for her. "Radio right now is strange all over the country," Melissa lamented in September of 1992. "When I came out with my new album, the rock stations said it's dance music and couldn't play it. And I'm not a hit-radio artist, so that format wouldn't play it. So [the album] kind of fell between the cracks" (qtd. in Britt, "Etheridge Softens Her Style").

So even with a Grammy under her belt, Melissa had to hit the road in order to broaden her fan base. The *Never Enough* tour was tailored to achieve that very end: it was a dynamic effort. Jeffrey Gaines provided a low-key opening set. But then came Melissa, Kevin, Fritz, and the rest of the band (guitarist Bernie Larsen and, partway through the tour, keyboardist Susie Davis, had been replaced by Rob Allen and Walker Englehart, respectively.) The star attraction, striking that infamous album-cover pose (shirt on, though), commanded the stage from the rear, her back turned dramatically towards the audience. The first few notes of "Ain't It Heavy" sounded; the crowd surged to its feet in a wave of response; Melissa swung around as the

lights flared and started jamming relentlessly on her guitar. The first four songs were played one after the other,
each flowing into the next, and this technique seemed to
drive everybody into a frenzy. "The Boy Feels Strange"
then allowed the faithful to gear down for a bit, only to
rev right back up again with "Chrome Plated Heart" and
"You Can Sleep while I Drive."

Later in the show, during "Dance without Sleeping,"
Melissa wandered dreamily about the stage, singing into
a wireless mike. "Keep It Precious" . . . "Let Me Go" . . .
then came the last four songs, which did a spectacular job
of pumping the crowd right back into its original state of
rock euphoria. During "You Must Be Crazy for Me," each
band member did a solo, and then the entire crew joined
Fritz Lewak at the drums. Melissa distributed sticks, and a
"group percush" on the drum kit ensued. "Bring Me
Some Water" followed by "Meet Me in the Back" pushed
them higher and higher. "Like the Way I Do" left them
dripping with sweat from dancing in the aisles. "2001" was
the first encore, but the real heart-stopping show closer
was the second, "The Letting Go." Melissa did it alone.
Returning to the stage, she played the piano softly, brought
the crowd back down to earth, and gently dropped them
off.

Etheridge was putting everything she had into performing, and it showed. She won new fans with every concert.
She was also gaining confidence. While appearing at a
festival in Amsterdam during the *Never Enough* tour, her
crowd-pleasing playfulness and genuineness surfaced when
Kevin ran into some trouble with his bass guitar just as she
was about to perform a song she'd introduced as new.
Another bass was found for Kevin, and Melissa asked, "Are
you ready?" Fiddling with the replacement bass, Kevin
shook his head. After a few more seconds, Melissa asked,
"Ready now?" Finally Kevin nodded. Then Melissa

addressed the audience: "Should I make him wait for me, for a change?" As the crowd laughed, she flipped her guitar over and began pounding on its back; before launching into "Occasionally," she announced, "This is not my new song; this is a song to make the bass player wait."

Traditions were being established during the *Never Enough* tour, as well. At Columbus, Ohio's Palace Theater, Melissa sang Janis Joplin's "Mercedes Benz" a cappella to commemorate something that had happened in Columbus on 28 March 1989, during the *Brave and Crazy* tour. Etheridge did a show that night at the Newport that was aired live on a Columbus radio station. The monitors kept popping and crackling during the first two songs, but then the problem seemed to correct itself. Suddenly, six songs into the set, right after "Precious Pain," the power shut down. Only Melissa's vocals mike was getting any juice. Unrattled, and with her disenfranchised radio audience in mind, Melissa marshalled the Newport crowd, got them clapping out a rhythm, broke into "Mercedes Benz," and pulled it off without a hitch. The power was ultimately restored, and the concert went on. Melissa has performed "Mercedes Benz" during her Columbus dates ever since.

Etheridge's popularity was burgeoning. Internet access was opening up everywhere. It makes perfect sense that an Internet mailing list was established for Melissa at this point in her career. (A Melissa Etheridge message board was also initiated on Prodigy at about the same time, in February of 1992.) The *Never Enough* CD liner contains a mailing address for info-hungry fans, but that fledgling fanclub never really got off the ground. The material it sent out was always out of date. The much-needed Internet mailing list was founded in Montreal by David Johnson and Glenna Vinokur; its official name is the Melissa Etheridge Mailing List and Fan Club. David had been a subscriber to the Indigo Girls mailing list and had noticed

*Melissa and
Bernie Taupin*

KEVIN MAZUR/
LONDON FEATURES
INTERNATIONAL

that as many postings to that list — even more, at times
— had been about Etheridge as about the Girls. He perceived a need and promptly filled it, starting out, in 1992,
with fifty pioneer members. Their ranks have since
swelled to over three thousand. The Internet MLE List
(its short title) has evolved over the years to become an
excellent source of downloadable Etheridge information.
It dishes up everything from a list of existing bootleg
recordings to a tally of all known concert appearances.
Would-be subscribers visit the list's home page at
http://www.ecw.ca/mle, and from there are able to
access all the list archives and download lyrics, a series of
frequently asked questions and their answers (FAQ), and
scanned images of Melissa — to name only a few treats.

Topics of discussion can range far and wide (this is cyberspace, after all) — from an analysis of Melissa's videos to what Melissa is wearing to what kind of car list members drive. Those who are happier avoiding that long strange trip can subscribe to the information-only list; just Etheridge-related content is received here — all off-topic postings are screened out by the list owners.

In 1992, a favorite theme on the all-topics Internet MLE List was Melissa's sexuality: Is she gay or isn't she? Many stubbornly defended Melissa's right to privacy; her sexual orientation was nobody's business but her own. She is definitely gay, others insisted, and her recent appearances at places such as Rhythmfest prove it — not to mention her labyris earring and her thumb ring. (The labyris is the two-bladed axe carried by the mythical Amazons; it's often worn by gay women, as are thumb rings.) Others flat-out denied that Melissa was gay and cited magazine and newspaper articles that refer to elusive "boyfriends." Mention was made of the large number of lesbians attending her concerts. Melissa didn't deny; neither did she confirm, exactly. Speculation was intense.

Then, in early 1993, one day after President Clinton's inauguration, the issue was suddenly cleared up. Melissa underwent her own inauguration — into a brave new world of sexual openness. She came out in style at the Triangle Ball, a gay and lesbian event. The press immediately picked up the story, and it made banner headlines in several publications. "For those of you at home who don't know what [coming out] means," Melissa joked later on VH-1's *Music Talks*, leaning towards the camera with a big grin on her face, it "means I came out as a lesbian."

It had been a long, slow process. But, of course, Etheridge's coming out had been more of a public ritual than anything else — if she had been in the closet it was a closet made of glass. Not only were most of her early friends and acquaintances well aware of her sexual orientation, but also she had never lied about it herself (except by omission) or asked anybody else to lie about it on her behalf. On one of Alix Dobkin's tours — sometime during the late eighties or very early nineties — she did a show at an Albany, New York, venue the night after Melissa had played elsewhere in the vicinity. Included in Alix's lineup was a song called "Lesbian Code," which runs through all the code names and phrases that lesbians use to identify each other. One of these is she's "one of us." After she'd performed the song that night, Alix asked her audience if they'd caught Melissa's show, adding, "Don't you just love Melissa?" The answer was an affirmative roar. Halfway through her next song, a cover of Van Morrison's "Brown-Eyed Girl," Melissa joined her onstage to lend a hand, and then stayed to perform a tune of her own. Alix introduced Melissa as "one of us."

For years, Melissa had been lending her support to various liberal causes, among them AIDS awareness and research and women's rights. Obviously, such involvements are no real indicator of sexual orientation, but it is true that if Etheridge had been locked up tight in the closet she would likely have avoided aligning herself with AIDS and women's rights activists, many of whom have been automatically labelled "gay" for their efforts. Among the many causes Melissa has supported, both before and after coming out, are Voters for Choice; Artists for a Hate-Free America; the fights against antigay legislation in Oregon and Colorado (she cancelled shows in Colorado to support the protest in that state); L.A. Shanti, an AIDS initiative; Women's Equality Day; and even Walden Woods. For this last cause, Etheridge participated in a benefit concert organized by former Eagle Don Henley, whom she had met while singing backup vocals with Edie Brickell on "Gimme What You Got," a track on Henley's solo album *End of the*

Innocence. The concert, which helped raise the funds necessary to keep Thoreau's famed Walden Woods intact

(it was under threat of being parcelled off and razed to accommodate shopping malls, and the like), was headlined by Henley, Elton John, Sting, Aerosmith — and Melissa Etheridge. She also donated her talents to support those battling pediatric AIDS. In September of 1992 she was one of the artists who appeared in a concert held at the Universal Amphitheater called For Our Children, a benefit for the Pediatric AIDS Foundation; it aired on the Disney Channel in February of 1993. On this occasion, Melissa performed a priceless rendition of "The Green Grass Grew All Around" with a group of children. Later that year, she sang "Silent Legacy" for "In a New Light," an ABC television special aired to promote AIDS awareness.

So, although most of those who knew her were well aware of it, and although the causes she had chosen to embrace implied it to many others, Etheridge's lesbianism was still officially her little secret when the 1993 Triangle Ball rolled around. The subject had hardly ever come up in her interviews, which had focused almost exclusively on her music. If it did get raised, she would simply move the discussion back to her music. Still, by the beginning of 1993, it had gotten to the point where *not* talking about her sexuality had become a more glaring lie of omission. The issue of privacy had been eclipsed. Melissa had begun to feel like a hypocrite: her music was all about being honest and true to oneself, yet here she was dodging direct questions about her fundamental nature.

An article that appeared in *Music Express* in May of 1992 was the deciding factor for her. A reporter for that magazine decided to push Melissa for a public avowal of lesbianism, and the tension his tactics produced radiates from the published piece. Driving home the fact that her audiences have a significant lesbian component, the reporter lets his readers know that the subject causes Etheridge to squirm in her seat. "[R]omanticism runs through the Etheridge oeuvre, which remains obscure about the object of her desire by being non-gender specific," the article reads. Is this intentional, the reporter asks, "considering she has a large gay female following?" In the following extract, it's plain to see that Melissa is torn by the conflicting demands of privacy and honesty: " 'The gender-specific thing again,' she says a bit nervously. 'No comment. I write very personally, so [my songs] end up very I-you.' Melissa shrugs off the notion that she's a role model for young gay women. 'Any strong woman today, whether she's a tennis pro or a TV star, is going to have a large gay following,' she says. 'My following is that much more emotional. My private life is very important to me. There are rumors and there always will be. I'd like to leave it ambiguous because any other way the focus gets away from the music.' " Determined to force the issue, the reporter ventures the question, "Wouldn't it help young gays find their identity by having visible role models?" Here is his answer: " 'Well, maybe in the future there will be [such models],' [Etheridge] says with finality, effectively putting an end to the subject" (Trakin).

Damage had been done to her credibility. The only way for Melissa to rectify the situation was to come out, and so she resolved to do it. She just needed to find an appropriate place and time to take the plunge. Like her friend k.d. lang, she considered doing it through an *Advocate* interview, but she rejected the idea after meeting with the *Advocate*'s Barry Walters. Coming out in the press to a complete stranger just didn't feel right. Off the record, however, Melissa was forthright with Walters: she told him she was sick of evading the truth (see Walters).

Meanwhile, Melissa had continued to root for Clinton as noisily as possible. He was elected president in November of 1992, and when an army of brash new Washington insiders rode into town in January of 1993 to take part in the lavish inaugural celebrations, Melissa was among them. After twelve years of buckling under to the repressive Reagan-Bush and Bush-Quayle administrations, the city rocked with jubilation and excitement. Scores of Clinton-friendly celebrities converged there, many of them intent on channelling that energy into beautiful noise. Melissa sang "Stand By Me" with Luther Vandross, Ben E. King, Jon Secada, and Shai. She loves to describe the experience. "Everybody was there — Diana Ross, Aretha Franklin, Ray Charles, everybody. You'd turn around and there was Jack Nicholson . . . . [but] if there was a big star, it was our new president. It was such an amazing show; it really was. There we were," she continues, "on the Lincoln Memorial, with the band and the crowd, and President Clinton was right up front, like almost on the stage. You could just look at him, and you'd sing to him and he'd nod and smile — he was lovin' it. It was great" ("Yes, She Is: Melissa Etheridge").

The night of the Clinton inauguration there were celebrations and balls all over the city, but among the best was the Triangle Ball, sponsored by three gay and lesbian rights organizations. The crowd of over two thousand attending the ball (held at the National Press Club) was wired and feeling powerfully free. Everyone was experiencing a strong sense of pride in community. At one point, Melissa found herself on a balcony above the crowd with k.d. lang and Cassandra Peterson, better known as campy Elvira, Mistress of the Dark. The festivities were being videotaped for posterity, and the celebrants had been showing off and making mini-speeches all night long. Approached by the roving video team, Elvira leaned seductively towards the microphone and flirted with the audience: "You know, I'm not a lesbian, but I could certainly be talked into being one tonight." Lang, never one to miss an opportunity to score a laugh, burrowed her face between Elvira's breasts. As the crowd below cheered, a beaming k.d. declared that coming out had been one of the best things she'd ever done. She stepped aside, and there was Melissa Etheridge, who spoke to the crowd about how inspired she'd been by k.d.'s honesty. Her moment had come, and she was brave enough not to blow it. Looking down from the balcony's edge, she said: "I'm just really proud to say that I've been a lesbian all my life." Exultant, k.d. grabbed Melissa, and the crowd went crazy.

Later, Melissa claimed that it had all been totally spontaneous, more a function of the atmosphere than of anything else: it "felt like I was talking to my friends, you know? People that I pretty much already knew" ("Yes, She Is: Melissa Etheridge"). Coming out also seemed a natural extension of Etheridge's expanding political awareness. She had met Urvashi Vaid, at that time executive director of the National Gay and Lesbian Task Force, and credited Vaid (the partner of comic Kate Clinton) with opening her eyes to many issues and with helping her make a commitment to social change. Susan Faludi's 1992 bestseller, *Backlash*, also had an effect. Melissa, who had already recognized the vital links between gay rights and women's rights, devoured this investigation of the 1980s backlash against the women's movement. She was fascinated by the way Faludi punches holes in the credibility of all those studies that "prove" the existence of such phenomena as a "man shortage" and a "climbing infertility rate" among working women, while exposing the hypocrisy that permeates the rhetoric of the New Right.

Turning thirty produced a series of philosophical aftershocks, as well. "I was never really politically involved at all until about the last two or three years," Etheridge confessed in 1993. "Then it was just this sort of awareness.

I turned 30 and started thinking there's more than just singing, playing, and having a good time. There's a whole world. There's a purpose somewhere" ("Melissa Etheridge: LN's Exclusive Interview").

Before she could come out publicly, Melissa had to confront those fears that had paralyzed her for so long and take control of them. The biggest of these fears had been that her admission would alienate people she cared about: "You think there's some big black hole you're going to fall into and that all of a sudden people who have loved you all your life aren't going to love you anymore." She offers others the benefit of her own experience: "And I'm here to tell you that *that* does not happen. If it did change anyone's mind about me, then that's their problem — and they weren't there for me to begin with." The same specter of abandonment disturbed her on a professional level, as well: "my exact fear was that I had been embraced by rock radio — which was unheard-of for a woman of any sexual orientation. So just as a woman, I was already breaking ground. I was dealing with that and thinking, OK, *if I come out, how many stations are going to drop me?* It's another version of the same fear — being dropped, being abandoned" ("Melissa: Rock's Great Dyke Hope").

The cone of silence had been lifted with great fanfare on that balcony at the Triangle Ball, and Melissa found she had a lot to say. In interview after interview, she described the experience of coming out, often searching for similes to do it justice: "Coming out was funny. It was like finally registering your car. And when it's not registered, you're always worried that every cop, every policeman is going to bust you. You've got that weight on your shoulders and you're always looking behind you" ("Melissa Etheridge: Rocking the Boat"). So Etheridge finally stared down all vestiges of that once-powerful fear of rejection. She would never again be ruled by it. This, one journalist concluded in 1995, "yielded a sense of fulfillment in other areas of [Etheridge's] life." Melissa herself added, "Honesty with yourself and others is very centering. If you can look inside yourself and ask, 'Who am I?' then you can be clear with other people. I believe good things can come from that" (qtd. in Zaslow).

Finally, coming out meant that Melissa's partner, whoever she might be, would have to do the same. It was Julie Cypher's turn to endure the spotlight. At this point, she and Melissa had known each other for about four years. Some attentive Etheridge fans experienced a flicker of recognition when they heard Julie's name in this startling new context: Wasn't she the woman who had directed so many of Melissa's videos? "The Angels," "2001," "Dance without Sleeping," to name a few? Fragments of their story began to emerge. Julie and Melissa had met on 23 August 1988, the second night of Melissa's first American tour. At the time, Julie was working as assistant director on the "Bring Me Some Water" video. She was also married to actor Lou Diamond Phillips, who had hit the big time with his portrayals of Ritchie Valens in *La Bamba* and a gunslinger in the two *Young Guns* movies. Before she was hired to work for her, Julie Cypher had never heard of Melissa Etheridge.

She asked about her new video subject and was simply told that Melissa was some "rock 'n' roll dyke" (qtd. in Carswell). Julie had worked before with lesbian musicians, and they had generally given her the cold shoulder — she was just another straight woman to them. Fully expecting the same treatment from Melissa, Julie was pleasantly surprised. Melissa turned out to be easygoing and great to work with. Julie is a beautiful woman with short, dark hair and glowing skin. She is also quick-witted, thoughtful, and articulate. No wonder Melissa was hooked — instantly. Later, Melissa listed the qualities that had so thoroughly

captured her attention: "I think I'm attracted to strength
. . . [and to] independent ability, you know, to [women
who] have their own career, have their own things that
push them on, [have a] wicked sense of humor. 'Course
I'm just describing my girlfriend is what I'm doing, so. . . .
Intense and willing to challenge and grow and push themselves and me. Yeah" (qtd. in Phoenix). The two flirted
gently throughout their first two-day video shoot. Then
Julie dropped a bomb. She happened to mention something about her husband, and Melissa was thunderstruck:
"She obviously thought I was as queer as they come," says
Julie (qtd. in Carswell).

Then came the furious backpedalling. Each woman was
still involved with someone else, and so they decided to
build a friendship that would not overflow into a romantic
union and undermine the structure of their lives. "It was
very difficult," Melissa concedes. "I had a huge crush on
her — HUGE!" (qtd. in Carswell). As for Julie, she had never
been attracted to a woman before; as she puts it, "lesbianism had never occurred to me until I met Melissa. Then it
occurred very strongly." But Julie's marriage was showing
signs of wear and she wasn't prepared to just walk away
from it. She wanted to try and make things right again —
or at least attempt to gain perspective on the welter of
conflicting and unfamiliar emotions she now found herself caught in. What followed, Julie says, "was a very long
two-year crazy period where we were both circling in our
own relationships, trying to figure out what we were going
to do" ("Melissa: Rock's Great Dyke Hope").

During that time, Julie continued to direct Melissa's
videos, because Melissa had told her that "she was having
a hard time getting directors to really listen to her and pay
attention to what she would like and what she felt about
the song" (qtd. in Etheridge, "Kansas Girl"). Their mutual
attraction never faded; it moved silently along with them,

just below the surface of their professional interactions. Finally, Julie separated from Lou in early 1990 (although they didn't officially divorce until 1992). At first, Julie's parents were puzzled at their daughter's actions — how could she have left Phillips for another woman? — but they quickly adjusted. "I came out to my parents at 24," Julie has explained. "I said, 'Mom, Dad, guess what? I've met the right woman' " (qtd. in Carswell). Her mother, Betty Cypher, took to Melissa right away, and claimed to understand the attraction; Julie's father, Dick, shrugged, "It's not that big of a deal. Besides, Melissa makes great pancakes!" (qtd. in Arnold).

After Melissa went public, she and Julie granted an interview to the *Advocate*. They were ready to speak frankly about the trials and tribulations they faced in becoming a unit. And how had Lou Diamond Phillips handled losing his wife to another woman? The interviewer wanted to know. No punches were going to be pulled here. Julie answered: "It certainly wasn't something he expected, but I don't think it threw him for too much of a loop because he's a very open and loving person. When he met Melissa he realized what a wonderful person she is. He could see how the two of us clicked so well" ("Melissa: Rock's Great Dyke Hope"). The *Advocate* has a specialized gay readership, but news of the interview still filtered through to shock jock Howard Stern. Voracious for sensational new fodder for his high-decibel talk-radio vehicle, Stern pounced: he dared Phillips to talk to him about his divorce from Julie on the air.

Even though Phillips had already remarried, Stern taunted him over the airwaves: "Lou Diamond is a big pussy! I guess that's the kind of publicity you don't want going around. It hurts your dating, like girls start thinking maybe you're bad in the sack!" (qtd. in "Are You Man Enough?"). The *Advocate* was quick to pick up the glove on Phillips's behalf: Stern's rhetoric made its editors angry — which, of course, was the general idea. Phillips had proven himself to be a bigger man than Stern, the magazine declared: he had let his wife go, and did not behave as though his masculinity had been threatened. Still, Phillips felt he had to go on Stern's show to respond to the accusations.

The media circus eventually played itself out. In a 1996 interview, Phillips showed that his feelings had more dimension to them — the flat stoicism he'd been credited with could hardly have been the whole story. Melissa and Julie's directness with the press had been unnecessary, he felt; furthermore, Julie's public admission that there had been trouble in their marriage had damaged the memory of the relationship they'd once shared. Although Cypher and Phillips have remained fast friends — they even lived down the street from each other in 1994 — and despite the fact that Phillips has been supportive of his ex-wife's new relationship, Phillips has made it clear that he blames Melissa and Julie for his victimization by Stern and others: "I felt [Julie] had no right to do that to me, that their coming out was their business, and there was no need to drag me into it" (qtd. in Frankel).

This aspect of their breakup, while it continued to rankle Phillips for some time afterwards, did not undermine one special Phillips-Cypher collaboration. Phillips agreed to star in *Teresa's Tattoo*, Julie's first feature film. This 1994 extravaganza is studded with more cameos than a Robert Altman flick: veteran actress Nanette Fabray plays a drunk; Majel Barrett, of *Star Trek* fame, is her sidekick; C. Thomas Howell is a slimy villain; Lou Diamond Phillips is a big-talking redneck; Kiefer Sutherland appears as a traffic cop; and small-screen sitcom star Nancy McKeon plays the friend of the lead character, Teresa, who is portrayed by alternative-film star Adrienne

Shelly. But that's not all: k.d. lang is hilarious as a born-again Christian who tells Teresa, "Yes, I had a sinful life before I found the Lord. But I changed my ways. And the Good Lord saw fit to give me my husband, Frank"; even Etheridge crops up briefly as a flashy, cigarette-puffing prostitute in a police station. Melissa also composed the music for the film, including the opening song, "I Really Must Be Going," and the closing number, "Do It for the Rush."

Teresa's Tattoo is campy and rife with lesbian jokes and insider references. It never caught on, and its director claimed that she hadn't really expected it to. The plot? An extended series of ridiculous misadventures: nerdy doctoral student Teresa goes to a lesbian hooker party where she is drugged by three men; she wakes up with a new hairdo and a tattoo; more bad men chase her; she struggles to disentangle herself from her pursuers, who think she's someone else, and to reestablish her identity. As *Girlfriends* magazine put it, "Imagine *Buffy the Vampire Slayer*, only a whole lot queerer. . . ." That publication also called Cypher "a genius" (Findlay). It was just a voice in the wilderness, though; *Teresa's Tattoo* was almost universally ignored by the press.

The film would probably never have been made if Melissa hadn't come out in 1993. Its humor, its content, the playful liberties it takes, derive from a world that Melissa helped open up for Julie. By coming out Melissa also lifted the veil of ambiguity that kept her fans from really penetrating the songs on *Never Enough*. Suddenly, "You Must Be Crazy for Me" could be understood as a song about the beginnings of Melissa's new relationship: Julie resisted the attraction between them while Melissa could see it plain as day. And the real story behind the enigmatic "The Boy Feels Strange" emerged at last. Melissa expressed it like this: "My lover, Julie, was married when she met me. She's now divorced, of course, and went through a long separation, but, um, there was a time when . . . she was trying to make her relationship, her marriage work, and I was, you know, going on, but we eventually came back together and said, 'Look, we want to be with each other.' " Her discomfort with offering the subject for public consumption coming through loud and clear, Melissa pushed on, anxious to get her true sense of things on the record. When Lou Diamond Phillips "realized that his marriage was over . . . then our friendship was very strained, and the song is a song for him. It's a song about his trying to . . . reconcile the loss of his marriage, the loss of his friendship with me. . . . And it's just all about him and my feeling toward him" ("The Only One").

Six

YES
SHE IS

Yes I Am was released in the United States on 1 September 1993, and debuted on the Billboard charts at number 16. The album eventually went multiplatinum — it sold over five million copies — and earned Melissa yet another Grammy, this one for "Come to My Window." Pop radio finally started to prick up its ears. Throughout 1994 and 1995, scarcely an hour went by on VH-1 without Melissa Etheridge blazing onto the screen. In May of 1994, Melissa earned the distinction of being the first artist in Billboard's history to hold back-to-back singles — "Come to My Window" and "I'm the Only One" — on the Hot 100 singles chart for more than forty consecutive weeks. Etheridge was bumped upstairs: she now played arenas and stadiums and sold out such jumbo venues as Madison Square Garden. The dreaded backlash against her sexuality never materialized (only a predictable measure of homophobic grumbling). What was going on here? Why was her career skyrocketing now?

Ironically, some media scribes pointed the finger at Melissa's coming out. It's the era of lesbian chic, was their cynical line, and Etheridge has pumped her story for all it's worth. One critic remarked that Etheridge was being courted for "high-profile interviews and cover stories [by] magazines that hadn't seemed all that interested in her before she announced she was a lesbian" (Ransom). Some accused Melissa, in her quest for fame, of giving sex-starved and trashy media outlets the green light to exploit her personal life. After all, if Etheridge wasn't using her lesbianism to call attention to herself, why did she title her fourth album *Yes I Am*?

Bitchiness was disrupting their thought processes. Melissa had been reworking the album's title track for years. She'd performed it at Rhythmfest as early as 1991, long before she came out. "Yes I Am" is a love song, not a lesbian manifesto. It's about embodying everything for your lover. The singer asks her partner if she is her passion, promise, and end, and then answers her own question: "I say I am. Yes I am." The song was to have been included on *Never Enough*, and that album was to have been called *Yes I Am*, but when the time came Melissa realized that "Yes I Am" was unfinished. She saved it for later. She knew it was strong material that would find its rightful place in her body of work: "What more empowering words are there than 'yes I am?' she asked during the promo tour for album four. But Etheridge was not too naïve (nor had she been when it came to the *Never Enough* cover photo) to underestimate the response that title would generate post–Triangle Ball. "Yes I Am" had a whole new slant. "I think that's going to be *the* question this year," she joked with Blazy and Bob on San Francisco's KOME radio: "is the title of the album a statement on my part?"

A prophetic quip. The most thoughtful response Etheridge ever gave to that burning question appeared in her 1994 *Rolling Stone* interview. "The title of your last album seems at odds with a political climate where people are defined by what they are not," observed her interviewer. "So few people say, 'Yes I am.' Did you intend this as a statement?'' In answering, Melissa focused on personal responsibility: "When I wrote the song 'Yes I Am,' I said, 'Oh, my gosh, I want to title an album that.' Because, you know, the song is a romantic song. It's about a commitment. It's also about obsession. But the statement 'Yes I am'? You know, if someone asks you a question: 'Are you an Italian?' 'Yes I am.' You are taking the responsibility for that. You are acknowledging your history." The interviewer persisted: "Many people think 'Yes I am' is 'Yes, I am gay.'" Melissa responded: "But I also hoped that it could encompass all the other things."

If Melissa's sexual honesty wasn't generating her newfound stardom, then what was? Some insisted the culprit was VH-1. *Rolling Stone* music editor David Fricke got right to the point: "You turn on VH-1, and it's like Melissa TV!" (qtd. in "She's the Only One"). Etheridge herself, when asked how important VH-1 had been to her career, did not hesitate to answer: "Very, very important. I'm grateful to them for making me sort of a central point of their programming. It opened me up to a lot of people who hadn't seen my videos" (qtd. in "What I Watch"). But how had Melissa managed to get the influential national video channel to behave like an offshoot of the Melissa Etheridge Fan Club? She hadn't. It was sheer luck.

Certain changes were taking place at VH-1 that coincided with the release of *Yes I Am*. The channel had always been perceived as the outlet of choice for the terminally sedate. Its viewers could rest assured that nothing more aurally challenging than the strains of Kenny G, Michael Bolton, Phil Collins, and Lionel Ritchie would infiltrate their living rooms. But uninspired programming led to uninspiring ratings, and expert John Sykes was brought in to revamp and revitalize. Sykes set to work identifying a whole new set of viewers for VH-1: "This is a brand-new audience," he announced. "We call our viewers MTV graduates because we want them when they leave MTV" (qtd. in Cohen). The channel was determined to attract "those 25- to 44-year-olds who have shaken off adolescence but are still not ready for Broadway [tunes]" (Cohen).

Older yet cooler acts (Tom Petty, John Mellencamp) were now welcomed with open arms, as were newer ones — as long as they weren't rap or heavy metal (Sheryl Crow, Hootie and the Blowfish, Counting Crows). Melissa Etheridge fit neatly into this package, and Sykes was very excited about her. "When Sykes took over, he said, 'Melissa's gonna be the one we break,'" recalls Steve Leeds, head of video production at Island Records. "In the past, Melissa was an artist without a home. MTV thought she was too milk and cookies. She's become so huge that MTV can no longer ignore her; now she's part of that mix as well. That would never have happened without VH-I" (qtd. in Cohen).

Tracing the mysterious ebb and flow of mass popularity can only yield so many speculative insights. Maybe the most compelling reason *Yes I Am* shot to the top of the charts is the simplest and most obvious one. It's a solid album that contains several radio-friendly rock-and-roll songs. If it hadn't been, no clever marketing strategy could have made it take off as it did. *Yes I Am*'s press kit included these remarks from Melissa: "From the moment I started thinking about this record, I knew that I wanted songs that would be really strong live, because that's where I spend most of my time — what I do most is sing these songs over and over. So every song that I started to write, that I even considered for the album, I had to visualize live and I knew this would be a very live recording." *Yes I Am*, then, is all about the spontaneous energy of live performance and it represents Etheridge's return to high-octane songwriting. Melissa has also explained that it "has ten songs and is inspired more by my first album than [by] any of the others. It's very organic, very strong — it has a lot of strong themes. I made an effort to make sure that each of the songs were written with passion, and that they were songs that I could get up and perform live and feel them strongly" ("Yes, She Is").

Yes I Am was made in an unusual way. To exploit advances in sound technology, it was recorded on analog and then mixed down to digital. This technique had the advantage of preserving the live quality of the music — as Melissa put it in the press release, she wanted the album to sound like "real music slapping against tape." Why not simply record a true live album? asked Musique Plus in 1993. Melissa answered that she did intend to release a live album at some point; the problem was that record companies tended to think that live albums had to be greatest hits compilations. Her career just getting off the ground, Melissa wasn't ready to rest on her laurels.

A certain technological wizardry was needed to record *Yes I Am*. Kevin McCormick had to step aside to make room for seasoned engineer Hugh Padgham, who had produced Sting, Phil Collins, David Bowie, Elton John, and Peter Gabriel. Trying to decide on a new coproducer, Melissa had gone to a record store and paced up and down the aisles, selecting an array of albums she admired. She then tallied the producers of all these masterworks, and Padgham's name came up most often. Although he had never heard of Melissa before he was contacted by Island Records, Padgham agreed to check her out. He flew to New York from London to catch an Etheridge performance at the Beacon Theater. Melissa live "was just amazing," Padgham marveled. "It was like, 'Please, sign me up now, I'm in the studio!' "

Padgham agreed whole-heartedly that Melissa came across best as a live performer. The whole team would work together to ensure that *Yes I Am* had a live sound and feel. They would keep it fresh. Melissa was adamant that the fiasco that had been the initial recording of her debut album would never occur again. An interviewer mentioned to her that while Padgham was known for creating slick and polished products, he had seemed ready for a change when he took on Melissa's project. Melissa confirmed this, and added: "there were a few times in the studio where we'd be kind of stuck and [Padgham would] say, 'There's a lot of tricks I can do, but I don't want to do any of them.' I really appreciated that." Etheridge's main objective in hiring Padgham had been "to bring in someone from outside the family — outside the core that I'd been working with." She had sought and found someone "who wouldn't change things, but add to it and make it much more clear and better-sounding" ("A Fresh Out Look").

So while recording methods were kept clean and simple, a few top-flight sidemen were brought in to complement Fritz's drumming and Kevin's bass guitar. Lead guitarist Waddy Wachtel was back on the roster, along with keyboardist Scott Thurston, and organist Ian McLagan (contributing to "I Will Never Be the Same"). Also, two new hands came on board: Pino Palladino played additional bass on four tracks, and James Fearnley of the Pogues played accordion on "Talking to My Angel."

Yes I Am was recorded in roughly ten weeks. It was done "in what I call an 'old school' way," comments Padgham: just "four or five musicians in the studio with me and my assistant. It is just one, two, three play." Melissa came into the studio with her songs essentially completed, and all Padgham had to do was come up with minor suggestions, such as making a guitar solo eight bars instead of sixteen. "She's always got all the lyrics to the song finished and it is pretty much 90% sorted out structurally as well," Padgham elaborates. "Then we discuss the sort of dynamics of the songs and how they should grow. What is brilliant

Playful Melissa
BETH GWINN / RETNA

about her songwriting is that she has a real feel for what's right."

Protecting that fragile aura of spontaneity remained Etheridge's first priority: if a song didn't come together to her satisfaction after only a few takes, she'd move on to another; she would later return to the cut that had refused to gel with renewed energy and focus. To do otherwise would be to allow herself to get bored with a song — and to let that song get overworked. Fortunately, says Padgham, Melissa "just gives it all. Seven times out of ten, it is usually the first take when she goes into the studio that is the best." Massaging the process along from the producer's chair, Padgham hit on the idea of creating the illusion for Melissa that she was really giving a live performance as they were recording. He exchanged her highly sensitive studio mike for a regular stage mike so that she could treat the device the way she always did onstage. She could stand close to it and "holler into it and knock it around," Melissa told Rockline in October of 1993, and yet the quality of the finished product was as high as it would have been if she'd used a studio mike.

Virtually every track on *Yes I Am* stands out in one way or another. The first cut, "I'm the Only One," was the first single released from the album, but, typically, it didn't have any impact on the pop charts. Instead, it flourished on the rock charts. The third track, "Come to My Window," was the next single released, and suddenly the ice was broken: Melissa now had her very first pop-radio hit. Island quickly rereleased "I'm the Only One," and it followed "Come to My Window" onto that newly broken ground: the two songs actually competed with one another on the pop charts. "I'm the Only One" is vintage Melissa Etheridge, which is probably why she released it first. It's about the fear of being betrayed by a lover whose eyes are beginning to search for "something new."

In 1995, for *Musician* magazine's "How I Wrote That Hit Song" feature, Etheridge penned a short piece about "I'm the Only One." It was one of those "gift" songs: a tune that came into being in the course of a single day. That day was spent on the tour bus, where Etheridge has done quite a bit of her songwriting: "I believe I started [the song] in Austria, going to Vienna," she writes. "Of course it then takes weeks after to polish it up, but the bulk of it came 'boom' — the melody, and the idea of the chorus." She wanted to keep "I'm the Only One" simple. The verses would "paint the picture of the feeling of desperation, and then the choruses [would] give a strong, powerful answer to the verses." The bluesy beat of the song would recall "Bring Me Some Water." Summing up,

Etheridge pondered the source of the song's wide appeal: "I think people relate to emotion, pure and true emotion, the *soul*. We don't have enough of that in our day-to-day lives, and I think people go towards that. I think that's the appeal of 'I'm the Only One' . . . . I was excited to perform it live. I felt like in concert it would really grab people. And it has."

The "I'm the Only One" video grabbed people, too. Steamy and smouldering and sexual, directed by David Hogan, starring Brian Wimmer of the television series *China Beach*, the clip was filmed in a Los Angeles garage. It's set in a bar. Etheridge and her band perform in the background while women — straight *and* gay — and men drink, cruise, and dance. A dark-haired woman with short hair asks a blonde woman in white to dance, and as they begin to enact a sensual, rhythmic series of movements, Wimmer's character stalks over and cuts in. The dark-haired woman then retreats to her cruising spot against the wall and stares longingly at the couple on the dance floor. Wimmer and the woman in white kiss passionately.

Once again, controversy was guaranteed. Melissa was charged with permitting Hogan to exploit her lesbianism for commercial purposes. Supporters of this accusation claimed that the video perpetuates some damaging attitudes towards homosexuality. To begin with, it misrepresents the scope of sexual variation: male-female couples are in evidence, as are female-female couples, but male-male unions are conspicuously absent. Since lesbian images are standard tools of the trade for pornographers eager to titillate that very large and lucrative market segment comprised of heterosexual men, many wondered if the video, instead of displaying its creators' openness to all sexual orientations, was simply pandering to the mainstream. It's a common and irritatingly persistent myth that most lesbians would be reborn as heterosexuals if they could just find the right man. The same dissenters insisted that the "I'm the Only One" video — from the moment the woman in white steps away from her dark-haired dance partner into Wimmer's arms — is just another exercise in myth-building.

But, of course, not everybody saw the clip in this negative light. After all, at the *very* end the woman in white slips away from her male partner and glances in the direction of the wall. And the watchdog organization Gay and Lesbian Alliance Against Defamation (GLAAD) did present Melissa with its 1995 Media Award, citing the positive and striking lesbian images that abound in "I'm the Only One." Etheridge's own view on this? The video "is really open to interpretation. Each of the characters are cheating on somebody else at that time. It's about infidelity, fear of betrayal, and what the lines of sexuality are. . . . I'd much rather be titillated than taught this is what it should be, man-woman, woman-man, woman-woman" (qtd. in Carswell).

"Silent Legacy" is Etheridge's favorite cut on *Yes I Am*. It recounts an experience that did not involve her personally, so in that sense it represents a thematic departure for her. Based on a story her tour-bus driver told her, the song is a response to the situation of a very young girl thrown out of her home by her parents when they discover she's had sex. The anger the story first aroused in Etheridge hasn't subsided: "How come we, in this day and age, just say, 'Don't do it,' when we know what we went through as teenagers?" she demands. "*We* know how hard it is. *We* know how the world seems and feels, and how our parents never talked to us about anything. And why do we pass this on? It just — it makes me crazy! I grew up in the Midwest where nobody talked about [sex], and you just learned it as you went along, and in this day and age that's dangerous" (qtd. in Phoenix).

Elsewhere she has railed: "It's so medieval the way that we're taught that sex is dirty. It's reality, it's human nature. And it's what we will have to face as far as what we hand down to our children. We'll have to do some serious digging first to try to get at it — and to break the power of this way of thinking that is really never discussed" ("A Fresh Out Look"). "Our culture," Etheridge says, linking the fate of her song's lonely child to a long tradition of thwarted natural urges, "has really denied sexuality of any kind for hundreds and hundreds of years, saying, you know, 'Sex is bad, save it for someone you love, save it until you're married.' This denial is really a power thing. . . . I think if we are to evolve, and get out of a lot of the problems that we have now, we have to take a serious look at our attitude toward sexuality" ("Melissa Etheridge," *San Jose Mercury News*).

The song, then, is about shattering the generations-old legacy of silence within families. At the end of "Silent Legacy," we are urged to remember that much of what we've been taught is based on fear and told that we must refuse to pass this legacy on to our children. Melissa's empathy with the young girl she's singing about arises from her own experiences: while she was growing up, sex, much less homosexuality, was never discussed openly in her home. "My mother didn't say a word to me," Melissa recalls. "It was, you know, just don't do *it*. Then every feeling I had was confusing — my body was totally on fire, my mind was spinning and not understanding" ("Yes, She Is").

On *Yes I Am*, Melissa challenges herself vocally more than she does on any other album. Performing "Silent Legacy" in the recording studio, she accessed "a part of me that I hadn't opened up before": the soaring note she strikes at the end of the song "came as a complete surprise — and a total release. When we originally rehearsed the

song, I had planned to have it just fade out at the end. But
when we were recording it, it took on a life of its own.
Kevin, Fritz, and I brought it down real low and then we
just hit back up into the beat. It was just one of those
magic moments and there it was and we ended it really
strong" ("A Fresh Out Look").

Yes I Am includes another track with political overtones:
the rock anthem "All American Girl." A cocktail waitress,
struggling to make her way "in this man's world," finds
that her work weighs upon her more and more heavily as
each day passes. The tips seem to be getting smaller and
smaller. She wakes up every morning with a headache and
reaches for decaf and a cigarette. Her lover stays out all
night. Her best friend tells her he's HIV positive. An early
version of "All American Girl" turned up on an Etheridge
bootleg called *Being Sensitive*, a compilation of private
demos circa 1986 to 1993. In the earlier "All American
Girl," the heroine waits on tables at a corner café. Though
her feet hurt because she's on them all day, she always
breaks loose when her shift is over. She's a woman with
dreams, yet by the end of the song, four years have passed
and she's gone nowhere. She still hangs onto her dream.

"All American Girl" was never released as a single in the
United States, but a video was made of it. Directed by Tim
Royes, the clip aired occasionally on VH-1. A performance
format was chosen for the video, and it was filmed in
February, shortly after Melissa's new tour band got together, as they played a practice concert under the alias
"the Ridge" at the legendary Whiskey in Los Angeles.
Also, the National Institute on Drug Abuse (NIDA)
chose the song as the soundtrack for the public-service-
announcement video it produced as part of its "Get High.
Get Stupid. Get AIDS." campaign. In this clip, brief segments of Melissa singing are interspersed with episodes
of an animated storyline: a young woman gets intoxicated,

lets down her guard, has unprotected sex, and later finds out her casual lover is HIV positive. Susan Lachter David of NIDA remarked: "Young people today are naturally cynical. So when you're working with a celebrity, it has to be someone who has a sense of credibility with the audience." The institute selected Melissa as its musical mouthpiece because she "speaks from the heart, and in her own words; [she] carries a message that sounds so real. It makes for a unique and special kind of communication" (qtd. in Russell).

One more *Yes I Am* cut inspired a video: "If I Wanted To." The song was released as the album's third and last single in February of 1995, and explores the feeling of being trapped by the immensity of love but still wanting

Melissa during the Yes I Am *tour, summer 1995*
PETE WILLIAMS

to endure that fate above all others. The "If I Wanted To" video features a leather-clad Melissa playing her guitar surrounded by lightbulbs suspended from the ceiling. Text that resembles graffiti scribbles rolls past, and occasionally the video cuts away momentarily to images of various women. Two other equally intense tracks on the album that take love as their theme are "Ruins" and "Resist." In "Ruins," Etheridge sings of a failed relationship; in the promo material for *Yes I Am*, Melissa refers to it as a song about "digging into my past to try to heal my present." "Resist," she says, is simply about "infatuation and a first kiss" (qtd. in Beebe).

"Talking to My Angel" is *Yes I Am*'s last track. It has puzzled some listeners because in it Melissa identifies her "angel" as male. But their confusion isn't caused by any impulse on Etheridge's part to slide back into sexual ambiguity in her work; it arises from the assumption that "Talking to My Angel" is yet another meditation on romantic love. It's not. On one level, Melissa has explained, the angel of the song represents the spirit of loved ones she has lost through death — most notably her father and her grandmother. These spirits or angels reassure the singer that she's safe; she'll be fine. On another level, "Talking to My Angel" is about leaving Leavenworth and moving to Los Angeles. The angel is the artist's muse, an entity that encourages her and sustains her in her desire to continue performing. "I use the term angel to describe that higher, spiritual self that's apart from the physical self," Etheridge elaborates. "So when I'm talking to my angel, I'm talking to my beliefs, the inspiration. That's a very clear, powerful energy that you can use and draw from. When I'm onstage I'm caught up in that energy" (qtd. in Finaly).

Yes I Am's fifth track, "I Will Never Be the Same," is there at the insistence of Etheridge's fans. Although it was written for the soundtrack of the film *Welcome Home, Roxy Carmichael* — which stars Winona Ryder — "I Will Never Be the Same" never made it onto the soundtrack album (neither did another song Etheridge wrote for the movie, "Don't Look at Me," which remains unfinished). Fans kept calling for "I Will Never Be the Same" during her concerts, and many wanted to know why Melissa hadn't included it on an earlier album: "So many people wanted that song on a record," she says. "When I didn't put it on *Never Enough*, I was constantly asked, 'Where is it?' But it wouldn't have worked on that album . . . it fits really fine on [*Yes I Am*] — especially the way we did it" ("A Fresh Out Look"). Melissa once joked on television's morning coffee klatch, *Regis and Kathie Lee*, that "I Will Never Be the Same" is her "spin-cycle" song. Before settling down to write it, she put a load of laundry in the machine. Within half an hour, she reemerged from her workroom with "I Will Never Be the Same" substantially completed. The laundry was just entering the spin cycle.

On a more serious note, Etheridge reveals the song was written at a time when she believed that she and Julie weren't going to make it: "I felt [the relationship] just wasn't going to happen and I'd have to give it up. I wrote the song with that spirit in mind; I'm glad it happened, but it's gone. Fortunately, it didn't work out that way, and Julie and I are still together. I wrote ['I Will Never Be the Same'] in the beginning of that relationship" ("Melissa Still on the Road").

But of all the cuts on *Yes I Am*, the one that has truly struck the most resounding chord in millions of listeners is the third. In "Come to My Window," the singer cajoles her lover to come to the window and wait there in the moonlight; she will be home soon. Something is wrong. A chasm has opened between the two lovers, and pain seeps in. The singer needs her lover in her blood, and will sacrifice anything just to reconnect with her. On a very literal level this is a song for Julie written by a lonely and homesick Melissa while on tour. But "Come to My Window" can also be read as a reflection on communication and miscommunication: sometimes the best way to make oneself understood is not the most direct way. If you can't get inside by passing through the door, then look for an open window.

The "Come to My Window" video was the first Etheridge clip to make it onto VH-1's heavy-rotation list. Samuel Bayer was the director this time around. Bayer had done Nirvana's frenetic, rough-edged "Smells Like Teen Spirit" video, and in so doing had commanded the attention of many people, Melissa among them. Eager to push the medium of video further than she had before, Etheridge considered "Come to My Window" an ideal vehicle. She communicated to Bayer that there was a dark side to the song, an intensity that she wanted to capture visually. When Bayer came up with the concept of a lone woman in a room, Melissa clicked almost instantly on Juliette Lewis, who had been catapulted to Hollywood brat-pack status by virtue of her electrifying performance in the remake of the film *Cape Fear*. Etheridge had recently met Juliette: she had dated a friend of Etheridge's — actor Brad Pitt. Juliette was a fan of Melissa's, and when asked to participate in the video she jumped at the opportunity. The video production team just put Juliette in a room and played the song; the actress had gone in with a basic idea of what she wanted to do, and had ad-libbed her way through the take without benefit of a script.

The day before, Melissa had filmed the performance segments of the video. Judy Troila, vice-president of video production at Island Records, was on the set while the clip was being shot. She reports that rather than lip-synching "Come to My Window," Melissa actually performed the song live a number of times in a variety of ways. "It was like being at a show," Troila remarked. "Melissa's live performance really moves people and you get so much energy from it."

In the final product, we see Juliette in a cell; the only furniture is a bed. Bandages circle Juliette's wrists. She mutters the first several lines of "Come to My Window," and it's instantly apparent that she is mentally disturbed. We switch to Melissa, who begins to perform the song. This pattern of alternation continues throughout the video, and its effect is to create the impression that Etheridge is attempting to soothe the anguished Juliette with her song. Juliette paces, scribbles on the floor with a crayon, grimaces, and yells at an imaginary antagonist. As the song concludes, however, we witness Juliette sleeping peacefully on her bed. The camera zooms in on her wrists. The bandages have disappeared, and there is no sign of scars.

Yes I Am is strong stuff, both thematically and technically. The critics reacted to its mature artistry by trotting out all their most potent adjectives. *Stereo Review* called it "a hard-charging, heart-on-sleeve quest for the state of determined self-affirmation embodied in its title." Furthermore, the compilation "is at times reminiscent of a good midperiod Stones album, its tunes building a steady head of steam as bluesy guitar figures curl with increasing fervor around Etheridge's mounting vocal attack" (Puterbaugh 126). *Outlines*, Chicago's gay and lesbian monthly, raved that *Yes I Am* "rocks and rollicks with [Etheridge's] trademark urgency and lust-tinged reckless abandon," and declared the album "a celebration of love, desire, and living freely." The *Outlines* reviewer then added that *Yes I Am* "combines the best elements artistically of all three of her previous releases" (Bergquist). *Q* gave *Yes I Am* three stars, maintaining that it was more "accomplished" and that Etheridge's vocals were "more upfront" than ever before (Aizlewood). Inevitably, some longtime supporters felt that the album was too slick, but new fans were flocking to Etheridge's concerts in droves.

The release of *Yes I Am* dovetailed with the enormous surge in Melissa's popularity in the United States. It was a perfect time to launch a new fan club. Sealed inside each *Yes I Am* CD was a slip of paper announcing the launch of the "Melissa Etheridge Information Network" (MEIN, pronounced "mine"). For a membership fee of $17, Etheridge-ites could "keep up-to-date on all Melissa Etheridge news and events." They would be given the opportunity to buy preferred-seating tickets for her concerts, receive a free subscription to the Melissa Etheridge newsletter, and have first choice of "exclusive" Melissa Etheridge merchandise. Pretty hokey, some objected. Greg Kinnear couldn't resist teasing Melissa about it during a 1994 televised interview, even putting in a call to MEIN while they were on the air. Melissa sat across from him, simultaneously moaning, blushing, and laughing. She must have been profoundly relieved that Kinnear couldn't get through.

But the establishment of MEIN did more than give a few pesky interviewers an excuse to tease Melissa; it also opened a familiar can of worms. Suddenly the accusations were flying again: Melissa was trying to squeeze more money out of her fans; she had gone commercial; she had been corrupted by her money-grubbing record company. Forced to justify herself, she explained that all member dues were channeled back into MEIN, which then dispensed the funds to the company that actually ran the network. The company covered salaries, printer's bills, postage, and so on. She also pointed out that the original proposal for the network had called for a 900 line to be set up: Melissa had nixed that idea, opting to skim no profit

Melissa during
the Yes I Am
tour, summer 1995
PETE WILLIAMS

at all from calls to MEIN (the network's hotline is not
a toll-free number, though; callers sustain regular long-
distance charges). Melissa went on to declare that the only
aspect of MEIN that put *any* money in her pocket was
merchandising. This was fair, she insisted.

What had really sold Etheridge on the network idea,
though, was that it was a way to provide her most avid fans
with preferred seating at her concerts. She had long been
disturbed by the fact that these people had to pay scalper's
prices if they wanted to obtain front-row seats, and was
wide open to creative suggestions on how to keep her
loyal supporters from getting burned. When the network
concept was pitched to her stressing the preferred-seating
advantage, Etheridge capitulated. Of course, it can still

be argued that MEIN tacks service charges onto the price of the tickets it sells and therefore does profit from the preferred-seating arrangement. And that preferred seating is not always so "preferred": some MEIN members have complained that the seats they get are nowhere near the front of the concert venue, and that their nonmember friends manage to procure better seats through Ticketmaster. This happens because MEIN is allotted only a certain number of seats by each venue. Seat assignments are made by lottery. Some members get great seats, while others are sent to concert-hall Siberia.

The *Yes I Am* tour, swept along on a wave of critical approval, drummed up a host of new recruits for MEIN. The spectacle was extended through the summer of 1995, and album sales continued unabated. Etheridge routinely astonished the crowds with her two-and-a-half hour performances. Her stage antics and innovations kept them enthralled. During "Silent Legacy," she would sink to the floor with her guitar and make love to it, sliding her body sensually across its frets and strings. She would conduct a mock telephone conversation during "You Used to Love to Dance." People who had never seen an Etheridge concert before were done in by the group jam on "Chrome Plated Heart." The drummer would tap each guitar with his sticks as each guitarist fingered chords; then the band would gather at the drum kit for a group percussion session. Another showstopper was Etheridge's cover of AC/DC's "You Shook Me All Night Long"; when Brian Johnson of AC/DC joined her on a Tampa concert stage as she belted out this anthem, it brought the house down.

What moved everybody most powerfully, though, was the solo acoustic set halfway through the concert. Melissa would vanish from the main stage and then reappear on a smaller stage located in the midst of the audience;

here she would proceed to perform — accompanied only by her Ovation — a set of songs that included "Ain't It Heavy" and "All the Way to Heaven" (introduced as a tune from an upcoming album). Music-industry trade magazine *Pollstar* judged the *Yes I Am* tour to be one of the year's biggest. Reviewing Etheridge's New Haven concert, one critic simply declared, "Talk about your fire and brimstone!" (Hicks).

The show was tightly produced and professionally packaged. Etheridge had moved into an entirely new career dimension, becoming, in a sense, an industry unto herself. She had learned to fly, but she had, in the meantime, been forced to cope with the loss of two important fellow travelers. Kevin McCormick and Fritz Lewak made a sudden decision to leave Etheridge and join Jackson Browne's band. Etheridge had little to say about it in the press, and MEIN had only this to report: Kevin and Fritz had gone over to the Browne camp, and both had done some studio work with Jackson before. It's not so difficult, though, to identify a couple of solid reasons for the defection. First, Hugh Padgham had bumped Kevin from the coproducer's seat on *Yes I Am*; second, both Kevin and Fritz had been over-tracked on a number of *Yes I Am* cuts. When asked how Kevin and Fritz had felt about this, Melissa replied, "Well, let me say: I have a whole new band." She went on to call the split "sort of political, sort of personal. Jackson can certainly offer [Kevin and Fritz] a lot more money right now. And they saw me changing and thought they would change, too" ("Staying Close"). It seems that the divorce was an amicable one: when the Rock and Roll Hall of Fame opened in Cleveland in 1995, the event was marked by a megaconcert; Melissa joined Jackson Browne and his band — including Kevin and Fritz — onstage for a rendition of "Wake Up, Little Suzy," and the only sparks that flew were generated by the performance.

Some have even ventured to say that it was all for the best as far as Melissa was concerned. One journalist remarked: "Perhaps having a new band forced the singer and guitarist to hear herself in a new light. . . . Etheridge show[s] a remarkable new emotional and dynamic range . . ." (Maples). It is true that Etheridge's new band harbored some exceptional talent. On guitar (and occasionally on keyboards) was John Shanks, a self-described "guitar nut." Shanks had accompanied Melissa on her first tour of the United States, after the release of her debut album. He sings her praises: "Melissa is so much fun to hang out with and to make music with . . . you feel that you can be yourself and take chances and not feel stifled or feel like you're walking on eggshells. I've worked with people that give you those looks that say don't overstep your bounds. It's not like that at all with her. She trusts you enough to allow you to do your best work" (qtd. in Zollo). Mark Browne was recruited to play bass guitar — a solid, sensitive, head-down-and-concentrate-deeply kind of performer. Mark, in turn, introduced Melissa to Dave Beyer, the inventor of RattleStix, who was invited to fill the void on drums.

When it rains, it pours. For Etheridge, 1994 proved to be one happy, sustained deluge. In February, she opened for Sting several times; joining the King of Pain onstage for his encore — "Every Breath You Take" — was a career highlight for her. This series of forty-five-minute sets helped to broaden Melissa's fan base, as did another short stint of nine opening sets she did for the Eagles in June and July during their *Hell Freezes Over* tour. Hundreds of thousands of people who might otherwise never have turned their attention to Melissa now had her front and center.

Also that June, Melissa — prodded by the indefatigable k.d. lang — agreed to perform a set at the Beacon Theater

Melissa and k.d. lang
Lifebeat benefit concert, Beacon Theater, N.Y.C., June 24, 1994
STEVE EICHNER/RETNA

in New York as part of a benefit for Lifebeat. The show, later televised on VH-1, featured such acts as Queen Latifah, Seal, Sarah McLachlan, and Jon Secada. Melissa and lang closed the proceedings with a duet of "You Can Sleep while I Drive." Just two days later, Melissa was honored in Los Angeles by VH-1 for her work with L.A. Shanti (an AIDS organization), and for the occasion she performed "I'm the Only One" and did a duet cover with Van Halen's Sammy Hagar of the Stones classic "Honky Tonk Woman."

There was no letup in August. Etheridge was named VH-1 Artist of the Month, and the channel put "I'm the Only One" into heavy rotation. On 13 August, VH-1 aired a "Roots Rock and Roll of Melissa Etheridge" special, which had been taped at Nickelodeon Studios in Orlando, Florida. In it, Melissa performed her music and talked about the artists who had formed her own art with their influence, among them Janis Joplin and Joan Armatrading.

The day this show aired was the day Etheridge took the stage at Woodstock II. She'd known that the concert, unlike its fabled predecessor, would be a media circus — an extravaganza of photo ops, record plugging, and souvenir hawking. She'd also known that Woodstock I was an impossible act to follow. Still, she wanted to be a part of it all. Later, she told Regis and Kathie Lee that she would never regret that decision: Woodstock II had turned out to be a phenomenal experience for her. "It really took a lot to keep grounded," she added. "There was so much energy and so many people that were so excited just to be there." When CNBC's Daisy Fuentes asked her to describe what it had been like, Melissa could only say, "Words like 'awesome' just come out." Getting to the Woodstock II site at Saugerties, New York, had been another adventure in itself. In the interests of security, the Etheridge bus had transported all hands to "a secret place," which turned out to be a Moonie camp. They were then loaded into a van and taken to a boat, on which they made their way down the Hudson River. Disembarking, the band piled into a second van, which actually took them to the concert site.

Once onstage, Melissa wowed the crowd with a set lasting roughly thirty minutes. She began with several original songs from *Yes I Am*, and threw in "Bring Me Some Water" and "Like the Way I Do." Introducing "Silent Legacy," Melissa uttered these words: "Don't let the people who live on fear and hate govern how you live." This advisory has been quoted many times since by inspired fans. Next came a medley of Joplin tunes — a tribute to the woman who'd galvanized the faithful at the one true Woodstock some twenty years before. The crowd rocked

Melissa performs during Woodstock '94
KEVIN MAZUR / LONDON FEATURES INTERNATIONAL

to "Try (Just a Little Bit Harder)," "Cry," "Move Over," and "Piece of My Heart." Pausing midway through this last song, Melissa inserted a Bette Midler-esque wisecracking digression on the nature of love. "Love is like that," she informed the sea of people before her. "Love can make you feel soooooo good. Usually it's in the first two weeks, but you remember those." She then ruminated on what it's like to fall in love: just when you've surrendered to somebody, when they've got you in the palm of their hand, "They say they want their freedom!" And they leave, taking the good CDs, the good cassettes, and the good clothes. But never fear, she said. One day they'll come crawling back and knock on your door. Now's your chance to give them hell, but . . . "I know you're gonna do what I would do." She added slyly, you're going to "look at them and say, 'Come on, baby . . . come on . . . take another little piece of my heart.'" As Etheridge sailed into the last verse of the song, the audience roared.

A month later, Melissa inducted Joplin into the Rock and Roll Hall of Fame by performing her own rendition of "Piece of My Heart." In a reverent speech that many numbered among the best of that extraordinary evening, Etheridge remarked: "[Joplin] was the only goddess in a sea of rock gods" (qtd. in Swenson).

As the banner year rolled on, Melissa continued to make headlines. She toured the White House with Julie in August after a show in Richmond, Virginia, meeting President Clinton and, by her own account, "choking" in his presence. She had been unprepared for the encounter. When she mentioned that her mother lived in Arkansas (Clinton's home state), the president naturally asked where. Melissa blanked right out; Julie had to supply the answer.

In September, Melissa and Julie were featured in a *People* article. The piece appeared in the Couples section of the popular weekly — not "the 'Deviants' section," as Melissa has joked. In October, Melissa joined a host of rock's heaviest hitters in Memphis, Tennessee, to pay tribute to the King of Rock and Roll. She covered Elvis's "Burning Love," and later explained her choice to television interviewer Greg Kinnear by insisting that she just *had* to seize the opportunity to sing "I'm just a hunka, hunka burnin' love!" In November, Etheridge returned to Leavenworth for the South Leavenworth Park benefit, and on the fifteenth of that month she sang the national anthem at Madison Square Garden during the Virginia Slims Tennis Championships. Her friend Martina Navratilova, tennis champ and high-profile lesbian, would be playing professionally for the last time, and had asked Melissa to lend her talents in honor of the occasion.

The year drew to a close with Melissa performing "I'm the Only One" at the Billboard Music Awards, held in December. The first major leg of Melissa's *Yes I Am* tour was concluded that month with a megaconcert at Madison Square Garden. It was a night to remember: MEIN members brought their heroine to tears by flicking their lighters in unison as Melissa began "Silent Legacy." "All my stage composure went *poof*," she admits, when she saw hundreds of tiny flames flare in the darkness (qtd. in Dunn, "Melissa Etheridge").

On 1 March 1995, resplendent in an outfit custom designed by Pamela Baresh, Melissa accepted her second Grammy for Best Female Rock Performance. It looked as though that fast train she was riding would carry her right through 1995, as well. She performed "Come to My Window" on the live telecast of the awards show, and when she had brought the number to a close she sprinted over to the podium to present four awards with Bob Seger, who'd serenaded her through headphones while she hid out in the family rec room as a music-hungry Leavenworth teenager. ("I'm the Only One" had also been nominated for Best Rock Song, but it didn't win.) On the twenty-first of that month, Melissa appeared on MTV's *Unplugged*. She has since been hailed as one of the few artists to do that show who actually grasped its original concept. She jettisoned all the bells and whistles and delivered a breathtakingly intimate performance to a rapt studio audience.

The segment was shot at the Brooklyn Academy of Music's Opera House. Etheridge was alone onstage with her twelve-string Ovation. Dressed in jeans, a T-shirt, and a blue denim overshirt, she did a set composed mostly of *Yes I Am* cuts, though "Bring Me Some Water," "Ain't It Heavy," and "Like the Way I Do" rounded out the selection of original material. She also elected to cover Rod Stewart's "Maggie May" and Joplin's "Piece of My

Heart." ("You Can Sleep while I Drive," "All the Way to Heaven," and "Occasionally" were all cut from the telecast.) The heart-stopping moment came, however, when Melissa's idol Bruce Springsteen joined her onstage for a duet of his "Thunder Road." It had to be taped twice. Melissa fluffed the line "So Mary climb in" during the first take because she had spaced out while trying to come to terms with the magnitude of the occasion. She'd been mesmerized as she watched Bruce perform, and had momentarily become his audience instead of his partner. Actually, Melissa admitted in an Australian television interview, she'd come close to forgetting to do the line during the second take, too, but Bruce had stepped back from the mike in order to cue her and she'd managed to get the words out just in time. The gaffe was not really noticeable to the television audience; but it does explain why Springsteen laughs as he moves away from the microphone and why Melissa grabs him, laughing, at the end of the song.

Melissa told Rockline in 1996 that *Unplugged* was "Absolutely the greatest thing that has ever happened to me, and it was an honor and a privilege, and I still get all crazy inside when I think about it." When setting up the show, MTV had asked Melissa if there was anyone she particularly wanted to do a duet with. "Springsteen," she'd replied without hesitation, but she'd only been half-serious. She'd been wanting to cover "Thunder Road," but it hadn't occurred to her that she would ever be granted the opportunity to blend voices with the Boss. MTV asked; Springsteen accepted; Melissa was struck dumb. Maybe Springsteen's acceptance was eased along by the fact that the MTV people popped the question at precisely the right moment: Springsteen had been watching from the wings as Melissa tore into "Piece of My Heart" during the Rock and Roll Hall of Fame Joplin induction.

The two meshed smoothly onstage. In Melissa's words: "He sang ["Thunder Road"] the way he'd been singing it lately, in a kind of Dylanesque, low-key way. But I was listening to the 'Born to Run' album version and singing it really hard. What happened was that I sang the 'Born to Run' version and he sang the new version and it just kind of melded together. It was interesting" (qtd. in Morse). Still, performing the duet was no easy task, despite the priceless result. Melissa later confessed: "I had learned ["Thunder Road"] in E and A. I sing it in A when I sing it. On the record it's in E. But these days [Springsteen] sings it in F because he puts a capo on and plays it a half-step up. And I *never* use a capo. I never learned. I never even understood why — just play it in F if you want to, just play it in the other key. So," Etheridge continues, "I had to learn it in F, and in rehearsal I kept going to D minor when I should have gone to A minor, because there's no normal pattern to the song. So doing that, and remembering where I was supposed to sing, and looking at [Bruce] singing and being totally blown away by being with him, made it a hard time. But it was the best" (qtd. in Zollo).

Etheridge's *Unplugged* performance left a good taste in the critics' mouths. *Acoustic Guitar* gushed: "[Etheridge] played . . . with a power and presence that only comes from many years in front of audiences learning how to wring every last drop of music out of steel strings and one voice." To most people in the rock world, the reviewer explained, "playing unplugged implies a kinder, gentler take on the music. In Etheridge's case, just the opposite is true. Although her records definitely rock hard, the band masks her charisma as a guitarist and, especially, as a singer. With a band, she's a rocker in the vein of many other rockers; by herself, she sounds much less conventional and far more dangerous. Rather than *unplugged*, a more appropriate term for her solo show would be *unleashed"* (Rodgers, "Unleashed").

Unplugged producer Alex Coletti was similarly impressed with Melissa's performance — so much so that he wanted to see it released as an album. Series veterans Tony Bennett and Eric Clapton, among others, had taken that step and their products had taken off, critically and commercially. "Yes I Am," "Bring Me Some Water," and "Occasionally" were Coletti's picks as the *Unplugged* album's singles. But Melissa said no. The idea of an *Unplugged* album was rapidly becoming a cliché, she reasoned; it seemed that everyone had done one. Also, if she went ahead with the project she wouldn't be able to put out another album until the spring or summer of 1996 (see Morse).

On 7 April 1995, Melissa deliberately ventured onto dangerous ground. It was time to reenter the political-correctness fray. She and Julie appeared in a People for the Ethical Treatment of Animals (PETA) ad — part of that organization's "I'd rather go naked than wear fur" campaign. The ad ran in the *Advocate*. Melissa and Julie were pictured together in the nude, though artful positioning of their arms and legs and discrete shadow manipulation ensured that their private parts were well concealed. Still, of course, all hell broke loose.

Public opinion splits over PETA. It's either a valuable animal-rights advocate or a hotbed of extremists. Those who adhere to the second view can get quite hot under the collar: witness the wrath k.d. lang induced in 1990 by doing an ad for PETA's "meat stinks" campaign. When her turn came, Melissa was specifically interested in protesting the fur industry's treatment of animals, and PETA was glad to furnish her with the in-your-face means of doing just that. But many felt she should never have aligned herself with PETA at all, despite the worthiness of her cause. As a

"We'd rather go naked than wear fur"

—MELISSA ETHERIDGE & JULIE CYPHER

consequence of the ad, she received some powerfully worded letters from AIDS researchers and activists — people with whom she'd fought shoulder-to-shoulder during awareness and fundraising campaigns — expressing their hurt and frustration over her involvement with an organization that opposed animal testing. Such testing is central to the search for an AIDS cure. Melissa, swayed by these diatribes, made the decision to abstain from doing such visible work for PETA in the future (although she did promise to support Julie if Julie chose to continue). "There was such controversy because there are so many gray areas," Melissa conceded ("Person of the Year"). She also asked PETA to stop using posters of the ad to entice new members; Etheridge fans had discovered that they could write to PETA and get an ad poster for a $15 membership donation. The offending article, long since pulled from circulation, is now a collector's item: some fans have reported seeing it for sale at prices as high as $150.

The new leg of the *Yes I Am* tour began in May. It was kicked off in April by a promotion dubbed Tickets First, and sponsored by VH-1, Etheridge, and Ticketmaster. VH-1 viewers were invited to call special Ticketmaster numbers on a given evening if they wanted to take advantage of the opportunity to purchase tickets and tour merchandise before they became available to the general public. The promo was a success: some forty thousand concert tickets were sold. Later, however, complaints began to filter through to Etheridge from fans unhappy with the quality of their seats, and she began to doubt seriously that she would ever participate in such a venture again.

Then, on 1 June 1995 she attained the crowning achievement. How do you know that you've truly arrived as an international rock star? You see your picture on the cover of the *Rolling Stone*. There, at last, for all the world to see, was Etheridge: attired for the occasion in gold lamé pants, black boots, and a black, short-sleeved shirt, she was immortalized as she sang and plucked the strings of a gold electric Gibson. An inside photo showed Melissa and Julie cuddling under a blanket and puckering up ostentatiously for a kiss. The article that accompanied these fabulous photos was written by Jancee Dunn. She begins with a description of driving around Los Angeles with Melissa in Melissa's car, a 1995 BMW 740i, and then offers her readers a synopsis of Melissa's slow, steady climb from rags to riches. Dunn spent five days hanging out with Melissa, and was able to provide rare insight into the rhythms of Melissa and Julie's personal life: a visit from Elton John; interludes of gentle teasing; dinner with comedian Ellen DeGeneres. Then there was a visit to the recording studio where Melissa — along with John Shanks, Mark Browne, and Dave Beyer — were laying down tracks for the next album. *Your Little Secret* was under construction.

Seven

CHATROOMS, CLOSE ENCOUNTERS, AND NO MORE LITTLE SECRETS

Ten seconds of "Testify" was all it took. On the strength of a few bars, Taylor Banaszak rushed right out to buy *Brave and Crazy* in 1989. She has been an Etheridge fan ever since. In June of 1994, Taylor acquired her first personal computer, and it came with a free subscription to America Online. Accessing the service, she discovered that a Melissa Etheridge message board had been up and running since January. It was a sluggish board — only a few postings were made each week — but as *Yes I Am* took off the chatter level began to escalate. A regular poster, "Raven55," suggested to Taylor that they start a Melissa chatroom.

The enterprising pair didn't encounter much difficulty. All they had to do was enter the People Connection portion of America Online and create the space. Then they had to populate it with the right kind of people. Taylor got busy searching the member directory to create a list

of users who had expressed an interest in Melissa Etheridge in their profiles. Her efforts yielded about 175 names.
Taylor e-mailed them all to announce the birth of the
new chatroom and to inform them about the Etheridge
message board in the Music Message Center.

During the second week of the chatroom's existence,
Raven55 proposed that they call the room the Ridge —
Melissa and her band had performed a few times under
that alias. Within a few more weeks, Taylor found that
the chatroom was filled to capacity at its meeting time of
Sunday nights at nine o'clock Eastern. The Ridge has
been mobbed on Sunday nights ever since. A nine o'clock
Thursday night session has been added, and Taylor maintains a list of some 1,050 Ridgers.

Etheridge was thriving in cyberspace. As the Ridge
began to cook, David Johnson's Internet MLE List buzzed
with activity. Celebrity impostors crop up fairly often online, and the conditions were ripe for Melissa wannabes
who craved the attention of a wide and affectionate audience. Most Ridgers, therefore (many of whom are also
MLE List members), rolled their eyes in annoyance when,
as July of 1995 drew to a close, they checked the Etheridge
message board on America Online and found the following posting from someone with the screen name
AMstudioB: "Hello. I know you are not going to believe
me, because I have said I never go on line. But I have been
in the studio for awhile and they have a computer that has
AOL, I have only one day left in here so I thought I would
get brave and say Hi. If you recall the *Rolling Stone* interview it reported me lurking [online]. I enjoy reading what
you have to say. . . ." Another imposter. But . . . there was
something about this monologue that seemed more
authentic than the rest: "I suppose you still don't believe
so I will give you some information that will come out
later so you will know it was me. The album will be called

Your Little Secret it will be released mid Nov. The single will be released about 6 weeks before the album which I'm sure will drive alot of folks crazy but it's a record company thing. There is a song on the album that I have not played anywhere [—] no one has heard it, it is 'I Could Have Been You.'" The writer then explained that her online access would be terminated that Friday night, but until then she would be happy to answer any questions posted for her. After Friday, her screen name would become invalid.

Of course, some fans reasoned, this "Melissa Etheridge" could be, say, an intern employed at PolyGram, which would explain how she knew so much about the unreleased album. So they administered an Etheridge trivia test: the would-be Melissa was barraged with questions — "Where were you spotted vacationing last week?" "Who were you with when you visited this place on this date?" All queries were answered promptly and correctly. Little by little, it began to sink in: this voice from the ozone had to be Melissa Etheridge herself.

Taylor was the lucky one who got the final confirmation. She had been in the process of e-mailing the pretender to the title, responding, with a strong measure of skepticism, to some questions that this proto-Etheridge had wanted answered by her fans in general. While online, Taylor received an Instant Message (IM) from this person asking if Taylor thought she was for real. Taylor replied, cautiously, that she was doubtful but hopeful. The two chatted for a few minutes and then her correspondent asked Taylor if she could call her to prove she really was Melissa. So Taylor divulged her phone number. Moments later, the phone rang. "My girlfriend was there and we had [the caller] on the speaker phone," Taylor says. At the sound of Melissa's voice, Taylor blurted out, "Oh, fuck! It really *is* you!" — and then, realizing what she'd just said, added, "Um . . . sorry." Melissa just laughed.

Over the course of the next day or so, Melissa posted her answers to the questions people were posting on the board, responded to the fan IMS and e-mails that were flooding in, and even sat in for an hour on an impromptu Friday-night Ridge chat. After Taylor "got over the initial shock," she realized that Melissa "was just like anyone else . . . down to earth and normal." And Melissa kept the promise that she'd given to online fans that one day she would prove in print that she really was the person they had been talking to: in a January 1996 *Advocate* interview she mentioned having gone online and described her phone call to Taylor (substituting Taylor's knee-jerk expletive with a simple "Oh, my God!"). Melissa also explained what had prompted her voyage into the unknown: she had been in the studio with her band, putting the finishing touches on *Your Little Secret*; during a break, Hugh Padgham had urged her to sign on to America Online to witness the cyber-chatter firsthand and have some fun with her fans.

Etheridge's fans adore her. The brand of attentiveness she displays — her online sojourn is just one good example — fuels their ardor. More than so many other superstars, she cares deeply about what her fans think and how they perceive her. In April of 1996, when another scheduled online chat fell through, Melissa posted an apology on the America Online message board. She rescheduled for the night before the American leg of her *Your Little Secret* tour got underway. Fans are forever telling stories about scoring backstage passes, meeting Melissa, interviewing her for small publications or college radio stations. Over and over, those who meet Etheridge echo the impressions of veteran fan Karen Leo, who encountered Melissa (for the second time) at Vanderbilt University during the *Yes I Am* tour. A representative for Rickenbacker guitars, Karen was delivering to Melissa the black Rickenbacker that appears in many of the promotional photos for *Your Little Secret*. "She looks you right in the eye," Karen remarks. She's "genuine, honest, and grounded."

One of Melissa's biggest admirers is Tim Dunker, whom she affectionately dubbed her "German Superfan" during a German radio interview conducted early in February of 1996. Tim, a native of Neuwied, has been to over sixty Etheridge concerts — or, as he puts it, he has seen "over 430,000 seconds of Melissa Etheridge live and [can] never [get] enough." Tim actually met Melissa in October of 1988, and has crossed paths with her many times since. He has an incredible story to tell. It all began on 21 October 1988 in Cologne, when Tim was only seventeen. He had tickets to see his favorite band, Huey Lewis and the News, and an opening act — Melissa Etheridge — who he'd never heard of before. When Melissa, Kevin, and Fritz took the stage, Tim, strategically positioned in the front row, "was really impressed" with "this little woman with this big, big guitar all by herself." The next day, Tim went out and bought Melissa's debut album, and then spent hours carefully translating the lyrics into German so that he could better understand what it was Melissa was singing about so passionately. "Sure, I didn't get the sense of every sentence but . . . being engaged in it so deeply gave me such a strong relation[ship] to every word and every note." Tim was hooked.

A few shows later, Tim showed up for yet another Etheridge performance. It was still hours prior to show-time, so Tim wandered into a little park next to the concert venue. In the distance, he spotted a woman sitting on a bench and strumming a guitar. As he got closer, he realized it was Melissa. He claimed a nearby bench, and just sat and listened. When Melissa paused to tune her guitar, Tim ambled over. "I said something like 'Hello Melissa, I really enjoyed the last three shows and I love your music,'" Tim recalls. Melissa asked if he was the guy she'd spotted in the first row; Tim confessed that he was, they talked for a while, and Tim garnered his first Etheridge autograph. At the show that night, Melissa made eye contact with him a few times. "I knew that I had to see her again," says Tim. When he did, the following summer when Melissa opened for Simple Minds, Tim was thrilled to discover that Melissa and the band all remembered him. And later, during the *Never Enough* tour, new band members Rob Allen and Walker Englehart made a point of introducing themselves to Tim, saying they had heard a lot about him.

Over the course of the next few years, Tim's habit of arriving very early at concert venues — a front-row seat was an absolute must — made him a fixture at such pre-concert events as sound checks. After the show, he would always wait around to catch band members as they were leaving: he wanted to say hello and collect autographs. Once, Tim, his girlfriend, and her sister wore the "Let's Get It On" T-shirts they'd had specially made, and Melissa and the band signed them. As time went on, Tim got to know such insiders as tour manager Uli Peretz (who hailed from Frankfurt), some of the security personnel, and Kevin McCormick. The Etheridge entourage came to trust and genuinely like the German Superfan. Tim would sometimes have to drive for hundreds of miles to see Melissa perform; unable to afford a hotel room, he would often sleep in his car. Crew members would occasionally slip him a plate of food as he stood sentry over his coveted front-row spot for hours at a time.

The night before Melissa's birthday in 1994, she played Hamburg, and, of course, Tim was front and center. Steven Girmant, Melissa's current tour manager who'd also worked for Huey Lewis and knew Tim from those early days, requested a favor of Tim to be fulfilled in Berlin the following night. Girmant had prepared a stack of flyers

that read "Happy birthday, Melissa" in both English and
German, and he wanted Tim to distribute them to as many
audience members as he could with instructions to hold
them up when a cake was brought onstage, just before
Melissa was slated to play "Similar Features." Tim managed to hand out about a thousand of the multicolored
birthday wishes. Melissa performed a short acoustic solo
set, and then waited for the band to return for "Similar
Features"; instead, Girmant appeared bearing a huge
birthday cake. The band and several crew members followed, and the crowd held their signs aloft. Everyone sang
"Happy Birthday" to a stunned Melissa.

In Belgium, two years later, Tim says, Melissa exacted
her revenge. As her Brussels show was winding down, she
made this announcement: "Belgium is the center of
Europe, Brussels is its capital, and right in front of me I
have a crowd from all over Europe. Most of you are from
Belgium. Down here are some fans from Holland, over
there from France, over there from Germany, and down
here is one fan from Germany who . . . I mean *I* have been
to every Melissa Etheridge show but right behind me is
him. And it's his birthday today, so . . ." Dave Beyer then
executed a drum roll as Melissa opened a bag of confetti.
"Happy birthday, Tim!" she said, striding to the edge of
the stage where she showered him with the confetti. After
the show, Tim was presented with an Etheridge T-shirt
signed by Melissa and each member of the band. How had
Melissa known it was Tim's birthday? Tim suspects it was
bassist Mark Browne, with whom he had struck up a
friendship, who tipped Melissa off.

Canadian Joyce Stoliar is another committed Etheridge-
ite who has lucked out when it comes to making personal
contact with her idol. In 1992, Joyce won a contest sponsored by a Calgary, Alberta, rock radio station. The grand
prize was an autographed Ovation guitar, backstage

passes, front-row seats, and a set of Etheridge CDs. From the time the contest was announced, Joyce relates, she hovered over the radio; she even had the "station phone number programmed into all phones I was ever near." Her perseverence paid off, and she was ultimately made proud owner of a beautiful black and gray Ovation, signed in silver ink with the motto, "Speak True, Melissa Etheridge."

The Calgary concert was held that night, and Joyce, of course, was there, installed in her front-row seat. According to Joyce, Melissa distributed drumsticks to each band member in preparation for the "You Must Be Crazy for Me" group percussion session. Grabbing a pair of maracas, she then approached the edge of the stage and looked over at Joyce, who was seated next to a security guard. Melissa, Joyce remembers, pointed right at her and said, "Excuse me, but this young lady is coming up on the stage." Melissa helped Joyce scramble up beside her, offered her the maracas, and led her over to the drum kit where she joined in the group jam. When it was over, Melissa gave Joyce a hug. The audience cheered. "It was the most noise that they had made all night," says Joyce. "I got back to my seat and burst into tears." After the show, Fritz gave Joyce his drumsticks.

But Joyce's story doesn't end there. In 1996, Melissa appeared on the *Tonight Show*. She performed "I Want to Come Over" and joked with host Jay Leno about Julie's penchant for collecting bowling balls and planting them all over the couple's lawn. Joyce, who was watching at home in Alberta, took all this in, and an idea began to form in her mind. She had just gone online and joined the Internet MLE List. It occurred to her that it might be nice to have an MLE List bowling shirt made; members could wear them to concerts and identify each other in the crowd. "I felt very close to these people on the list who shared my common interest," Joyce explains; here was a way to establish direct physical contact with like-minded people who had as yet only manifested themselves as disembodied voices. So, with some input from list members, a design was chosen and a raft of purple "MELister" bowling shirts was manufactured. Joyce met Melissa one more time. She sought her idol out at the Château Lake Louise hotel in Banff, Alberta, and made her a gift of two bowling shirts: one for Melissa and one for Julie. In return, Melissa resigned Joyce's Ovation because the original autograph had gotten smeared; she also signed Joyce's bowling shirt.

One of the funniest fan-Etheridge encounter stories is told by Elizabeth Elkins, who met Melissa in Birmingham, Alabama, on a sweltering day in late July 1994. Elizabeth had gone to the Oak Mountain Amphitheater to interview Melissa. The roofless venue did not have an air-conditioned backstage area, and the mercury was rising. Elizabeth and Melissa retreated to the headliner's dressing room for the interview. Elizabeth describes what happened next:

The room was lit only by small, rectangular windows set high on two walls. There was a modest dresser, a smaller than average sofa, and several chairs, which Melissa had draped with her clothing for the performance. She did not turn on the light: the temperature was already close to 95 degrees in the room without it. She smiled; I noticed she looked slightly older without the flattering lights and makeup of television and professional photography.

"Have a seat," she said, pointing to the sofa. I sat quickly, near the middle. She immediately sat down, much too close for my journalistic integrity. We recorded a few "Hi this is Melissa Etheridge and you're listening to . . ." to test my hand-held tape recorder and proceeded into the interview. I had about fifteen minutes worth of questions. I thought they were obscure and rather thoughtful: she acted as though she had been asked them all before — never saying "like," "uh," "well," or pausing to think.

So much for my originality.

As interviews progress, a reporter is often led away from the planned questions and into the realm of spontaneity. It is here that the best information is gathered. Melissa and I were about to enter that plane when I had a sudden realization . . . somehow, our lips were only two inches apart as we spoke into the tape recorder. Should I? Should I? Should I?

With a start, Elizabeth realized that Melissa was waiting patiently for the next question. Intent on Melissa's lips, her mind had gone blank. "Hold on, I totally, um, forgot what I was asking," Elizabeth stuttered. Actually, she admits, "my pulse rate was more of a problem." The interview lurched past this momentary obstacle and concluded without a hitch — but that was one kiss, Elizabeth now sighs, that she regrets not stealing.

Dawn Drier is an avid Etheridge fan. And an intrepid one. Her brush with Melissa, like Elizabeth's, has a comic dimension, and it also serves to reveal how thoroughly Melissa has rejected the star-attitude option. Some years ago, Dawn attended a multiartist concert in Orlando, Florida. There she won a T-shirt identical to the ones that staff members of the radio station that was sponsoring the concert were wearing. She made a daring decision: she would try to sneak backstage disguised as staff. Breaching the barricades without incident, Dawn wandered about without encountering anybody. She opened a door. There was Melissa, sitting alone. Dawn froze with her mouth hanging open. Melissa asked if she could help her. Dawn's mouth opened and closed, but she couldn't make a sound.

Melissa invited her in. Dawn managed to mumble a few words of adoration, apologized, backed away, and fled. Two years later in Norfolk, Virginia, Dawn got the opportunity to join a meet-and-greet line at an Etheridge concert, and thought she would use it to remind Melissa of her moment of madness in Orlando. But, when she came face to face with Melissa and held out a poster to be signed, Dawn was once again struck dumb. She couldn't squeak out a coherent sentence. Melissa laughed and drew Dawn to her for a hug. The combination of Melissa's hair spray and the perspiration on both their faces caused Melissa's hair to stick to Dawn's cheek, and as Dawn stepped back, she pulled Melissa along with her.

Of course, not all of Etheridge's encounters with her fans have been so positive. As everyone knows, in this media-controlled age especially, fame is a very democratic institution: virtually anyone can attain stardom (even talent isn't a prerequisite anymore), and stardom exacts the same price from everyone. Privacy. Take it or leave it. Melissa and Julie have had to give up their West Hollywood Hills home because too many fans found out where they lived and set up camp. And there have always been the stage jumpers — frenzied fans who are driven to jump onstage and grab Melissa as she performs. "It is actually *very* frightening," Melissa once remarked during a CompuServe chat. "I wish people would not do it." Elsewhere she has revealed that fans sometimes unintentionally hurt her in their urgency for physical contact; she's been scratched and choked and had her hair pulled. Melissa also fervently wishes that fans would refrain from taking off their clothes at her concerts and tossing bras or panties onto the stage. She has been smacked in the face by intimate apparel more than once. In concert, she's been known to crack, "You're going to need these things later when you go dancing!" ("Melissa: Rock's Great Dyke Hope").

Then there are the fans whose adulation crosses the border into obsession. "Some people have this sort of *Children of the Corn* look in their eyes," says Julie, "like they just want to grab her and throw her in a trunk and drive her away to be theirs" (qtd. in Etheridge, "Kansas Girl").

Kathleen McCrea, normally a levelheaded person, admits that she once got way out of line after an Etheridge concert at the Meadowlands in New Jersey. It was June of 1995. Driving around the deserted parking lot after the concert in search of some wayward buddies, Kathleen and a friend noticed that a tour bus that had been parked near the concert venue had begun to pull away. This wasn't the crew's bus; it was Melissa's bus. "This is the moment where I lost total control of reality," Kathleen confesses. "Sitting in my car, I had a complete conversation with myself . . . Should I follow . . . Should I not follow . . . So, I did the crazy thing. I attached my front bumper to the rear bumper of the bus. It was a go for broke kind of thing." She trailed in the wake of that bus all the way into New York City, where it stopped at the side entrance to a hotel. "Autograph," Kathleen thought. She instructed her friend to take their ticket stubs and a marker and stand behind the car; Kathleen positioned herself beside the car's passenger door. After five minutes or so, the bus door opened and Melissa came out followed by two "manager types," as Kathleen described them. Kathleen motioned to her friend, who then began to move towards Melissa. The "managers," now flanking Melissa, held up their hands, indicating to them both not to come any closer.

As she reached the hotel entrance, Kathleen recalls, Melissa "lifted her head and looked directly at me." At that moment Kathleen knew that she had "made one of the worst decisions of my life. Our eyes met and a long conversation transpired between our locked eyes. All of the energy, strength, vibrance, vigor, verve, zest, stamina, power, bounce, fortitude, grit, passion, spirit, and vitality that she exudes onstage was not present in her face and eyes. It's very hard," Kathleen continues, "to put into words the complete meaning behind her gaze at me. I know in my heart that she told me, 'Please . . . I can't give to you another part of me.' I can say, she was spent; she had given part of her soul to us at the concert." The moment passed, the hotel door opened, and Melissa was whisked inside. "I could see her small figure blend into the shadows of the darkened hallway," Kathleen concludes. "I would do anything to take back my poor actions and judgment," she says. "How much can we take from her?"

Many high-profile personalities have been stalked. Melissa is no exception. So when people approach her emanating a little too much energy, her internal warning signals start to flash. Two Etheridge supporters named Mona and Elizabeth tell a tale of meeting Melissa in the parking lot near the security gate after Melissa's January 1996 *Tonight Show* appearance. "We are Melissa fans; we love and totally respect her." Their behavior was consistent with this attitude: the two women were careful to keep their distance when they spotted Melissa's BMW. They simply held up a pen and a copy of the *Rolling Stone* with Melissa on the cover. Much to their delight, Melissa braked the car and, smiling, started to roll down the window. Then, out of nowhere, a frantic girl came shrieking up. She shoved a CD and a pen at Melissa, screaming, "Thank you, thank you! I love you!" She thrust her hands through the car window and began to paw at Melissa, "almost to the point of pounding on her," Mona and Elizabeth say. An increasingly apprehensive Melissa nodded her head, chanting "I know, I know, I know," trying hard to calm the girl down. When the crazed fan started pleading with her idol to sign her pants, Melissa,

Melissa signs an autograph for fan Mona Shield Payne
ELIZABETH HANDY

having already hurriedly signed her CD, refused. Looking frightened, Melissa quickly signed Mona and Elizabeth's things and drove away. Mona and Elizabeth remember that they "drove home, shaking our heads." They wonder if one day Melissa will have to stop giving autographs altogether.

Still, as a collective, Etheridge's supporters are a credit to her. Male and female, gay and straight, young and old, of every color and a multitude of nationalities: these fans are a testament to Melissa's ability to strike a universal chord. Sweep your eyes over the crowd at an Etheridge concert and you'll get a taste of what cultural diversity really means. As the concert draws to a close, you'll also realize the power of this one small woman: for at least three hours, all these people have been united by a powerfully positive energy. There is a healing aspect to such an experience.

That Melissa has helped and healed through her music is yet another reason for her strong appeal. So many of her fans can point to a moment in their lives when one of Melissa's songs captured their own emotions and helped them cope with a rough situation. One follower (who has asked to remain anonymous) claims that Melissa's music helped her to conquer the guilt feelings and the nightmares that had plagued her ever since she was raped at the age of twelve. She'd carried these demons with her right into adulthood. The priest to whom she had offered her confession right after the assault — the only person she told about it — admonished her, and ordered her to say a penance for her sins. Later in life, she says, "I was unable to confront or come to terms with what happened, so I buried it deep inside." Then, as a college student, she discovered Melissa Etheridge: "I could so much relate to her music. I could feel the music, and it really moved me. Her music had a very strong impact on me and I slowly developed the strength to trust again and to let [the past] go." Melissa, this woman insists, "composes her music from her heart, whether it is broken, feisty, or filled with love. I really feel that it was her music that softened my core and allowed me to reach deep inside and confront the situation and trust again. There are so many artists out there that write music and sing but don't actually say anything, but Melissa Etheridge is different."

Her fans have tried to pay her back in whatever small ways they can. For one thing, they hold listening parties. Marilyn R. Horowitz threw one of these at Rubyfruit's in New York City when *Your Little Secret* was released. All the Ridgers were invited. Everybody who attended signed a poster, which was sent to Melissa as an expression of gratitude. During the *Your Little Secret* tour, one fan hired a small plane to fly over the Jones Beach, New York, concert venue trailing a banner that read "Keep It Precious." For Melissa's thirty-fifth birthday, Internet MLE List subscribers put together a happy-birthday CD with clickable images, text, and sound — it even included a thirty-second QuickTime movie. Masterminded by Jess Breed, the CD

VH-1 Duets, *Doheny Mansion,*
L.A., October 10, 1995
NEAL PRESTON / RETNA

represented months of hard work. Accompanying it was a birthday card that had been circulated around the globe: fans the world over had signed it.

Etheridge, in turn, named *Your Little Secret* with such faithful fans as these in mind. She explains how this came about. Lurking online, she overheard a conversation between two of her fans. "One person was saying to another, 'Melissa Etheridge has really gotten famous and popular and successful now . . . she's no longer our little secret.' So I thought, 'You know what? I'm gonna put an album out called *Your Little Secret*,' because no, I'm not anymore" (qtd. in Nelson).

Yes I Am was a tough act to follow. Could Melissa surpass it — or even live up to it — with *Your Little Secret*? Would the desire to do that stifle her originality? But there was no need for Melissa to address such questions; she just refused to step into the pressure cooker: "Pressure's the kind of thing you create," she told Rockline in April of 1996. In fact, she said, the success of *Yes I Am* had boosted her confidence to such a degree that the prospect of returning to the studio with her new band to record *Your Little Secret* was a totally pleasurable one. No problem. Hugh Padgham returned to coproduce, and, at his suggestion, the phenomenal Kenny Aronoff of John Mellencamp's band played drums on a few key tracks. "I just went back in and made another album so that I would sort of feel like I'm still moving ahead and not stopping," Melissa explained (qtd. in Nelson).

The album's title track was released first. The single hit the stores on 9 October 1995, and the album followed six weeks later. An electrifying rocker, "Your Little Secret" is a playful threat to give away another person's secret and an invitation to share a sexual indiscretion. I know what you're thinking, the singer taunts, because I used to be that way myself.

The *Your Little Secret* CD was lavishly packaged. The first million released in the United States (and the first hundred thousand of those released worldwide, which came with a bonus CD of four live tracks) formed a limited edition. Structured on a keyhole motif, the CD cover featured six different and separate images of Etheridge; these could be shuffled behind a keyhole cutout to create six unique CD covers. If all six images were placed together face down, the lyrics on their reverse sides could be read as a larger image of Etheridge's logo — a combination of her initials and the woman symbol — emerged.

The "Your Little Secret" video picked up on the keyhole motif. Through a keyhole framing device, the viewer catches glimpses of Melissa and the band performing, models dancing, and even a shot of a young man wearing a "Brad Pitt Rules" T-shirt. The "I'm the Only One" video director David Hogan was enlisted to perform his magic on "Your Little Secret," and the result was equally provocative. Male and female models form a human wall that others struggle to scale; the climbers pause on their ascent to kiss and caress the wall people beneath them. Again, images of men with women and of women with women prevail: there are no gay men in sight. Melissa, dressed in leather, attacks a Silvertone guitar and emits a primal scream as the song ends. The clip is a visual feast. Both VH-1 and MTV ran it aggressively — that is, until it became clear that "Your Little Secret" was not going to be a hit single (although the clip was nominated for a VH-1 fashion award in 1996: Most Stylish Video).

"I Want to Come Over" was the next single to be released; it came out at the end of January 1996. In it, a woman yearns for her lover — very likely, the cut is a love song written for Julie. The "I Want to Come Over" video was shot in an old Los Angeles hotel. Apparently, when Melissa showed up for the shoot, she asked if the hotel was still in use, and the director told her there was a man living in one of the rooms. To ensure that the man didn't wander onto the set, he was given a bottle of Chivas. Gwyneth Paltrow (Brad Pitt's current girlfriend) is the star of the piece, and her performance echoes that of Juliette Lewis in "Come to My Window"; she also plays a desperate woman on the verge of a breakdown. She drives to her lover's apartment and sits outside in her car, struggling with her warring emotions. Sobbing, she shreds a letter, bangs on the steering wheel, and smears her makeup. As the clip concludes, we see her pull herself together and enter the building.

Your Little Secret's third single is the lovely ballad "Nowhere to Go." At moments, it recalls U2's "With or Without You," and Springsteen's influence pervades the song as well. It's about small-town claustrophobia — the Leavenworth variety in particular. Etheridge filled the tune with references to her home town: among other sites, the penitentiary, the old Veteran's Administration building, and the mighty Missouri River are evoked. Melissa contends that the boxcars referred to in the song were "really down there, and we used to buy really cheap wine and hang out there, because there was nowhere else to go in Leavenworth" ("Melissa Etheridge," *Us*). An interviewer asked her this question: "The song . . . contains the lines 'They never woke up / From the American dream / And they don't understand / What they don't see.' Do those words reflect problems you've encountered as a lesbian?" Melissa responded: "Absolutely. It comes directly from my adolescent feelings growing up in my hometown of Leavenworth and how people don't want to see. The small-town experience is especially tough on gay people" ("Anthem-Belting Etheridge").

To the delight of Etheridge's gay fans, Julie was chosen to direct the "Nowhere to Go" video. She takes a turn in front of the camera, too, playing Melissa's lover — not a great dramatic stretch. As the clip opens, Julie appears upset about something; she and Melissa get into a car and drive far into the desert. At an abandoned building (a mission?), Julie smashes a window. She and Melissa are then seen standing at the edge of a cliff, holding each other. Shot near Santa Fe, the video — especially its finale — is visually gorgeous. But it's all just a pretty illusion. Talking to VH-I's *Route 96*, Melissa explained that as they stood in their cliffside embrace, a helicopter bearing the camera crew circled above, and Julie, equipped with a walkie-talkie, was murmuring directions to the crew while she herself was trying hard not to think about how perilously close they were to the edge.

Your Little Secret is enriched by two more ballads: "All the Way to Heaven" and "Shriner's Park." "All the Way to Heaven," featuring John Shanks on nylon guitar, is about the desire to set a lover free. The singer dreams of driving around in a car with her lover, of going to a bar where they know the bartender by name, and of exploring a carnival where they buy cotton candy and sno-cones and frolic in the sawdust until they get thrown out. On VH-I's *Story-tellers*, Melissa admitted that "All the Way to Heaven" was actually inspired by a phone conversation she had once had with Julie. Julie had been depressed and upset and Melissa was far away and couldn't really help. She longed to whisk Julie away, take her to her favorite place, go "all the way to heaven" with her and make things right again. "Shriner's Park" is another tune with shades of its creator's Leavenworth youth. It's a more haunting song than "All the Way to Heaven." In it, a woman wonders about an old lover who used to go with her to Shriner's Park where they would strive to make sense of all they were experiencing. She also wonders whether her old flame ever felt crazy, and whether she ever got any answers through prayer to the questions they wrestled with. The singer ponders what would happen if she called.

One *Your Little Secret* song baffled everyone. "An Unusual Kiss" seems to be about a ménage à trois. Melissa has fueled the intrigue by refusing to discuss the song: "With this album," she asserts, "I'm going to start something new where I say, 'Yes, each of these songs is a part of me, each of these songs comes from a real honest place, but I'm not gonna tell you what it's about.' There's just too bright of a light shone upon my personal life that it's like, 'Uh-uh . . . you have to guess from now on'" (qtd. in Nelson). Melissa, burned by the fallout from Julie's separation and divorce, had understandably adopted a closed-mouth stance on things personal and domestic. Yet, "An Unusual Kiss," despite its author's suggestive silence, doesn't have to be understood as a song about a threesome at all. The taxi that pulls away at the end doesn't necessarily carry a third person; it could be empty, and the song could be the story of a nightlong struggle during which a lover finally decides to stay on after lovemaking — to stay on in the hope of building a committed relationship.

Your Little Secret also contains "I Could Have Been You," which Melissa wrote with John Shanks. Shanks, who has written songs for such artists as Joe Cocker and Bonnie Raitt, says that he shares his songs with Melissa all the time. "It's the Mike Campbell-Tom Petty theory," he explains: "If it's something that excites her, she'll run off. She heard my track for 'I Could Have Been You' on the bus to Biloxi [during the *Yes I Am* tour] and said, 'That one's mine.' The next day she sang me the song, and I got chills" (qtd. in Zollo).

For "I Could Have Been You," Melissa tunes her Ovation alternatively to E A D E A E, producing a sound quite different from that of any other Etheridge track on the album. The lyrics are a surprise, too. Melissa has regularly maintained that she prefers not to imbue her art with a lot of political content, but this song is clearly about the need to accept differences among human beings. She sings about the destructiveness of fear, and asks us all to show compassion and to try to understand and empathize with those who seem different, because we're all human beings. "I have had my own issues with fear," Melissa said on *VH-1-to-One*, a special aired prior to the release of *Your Little Secret*. "And I have had my own revelations about fear and how it drives this world." Probably Melissa's strongest statement ever about the issue of prejudice was delivered in the context of a 1994 interview with Daisy Fuentes on CNBC. Fuentes asked Melissa what bothered her most about society, and Melissa replied: "How some people have allowed fear to run their lives . . . and in return they turn that fear into hatred and bigotry and attack people." "I Could Have Been You" is an eloquent plea, directed towards us all, to break that bitter cycle.

The three remaining tracks on *Your Little Secret* are the rockers "I Really Like You" and "Change," and the final track, "This War Is Over." "Change," like "Yes I Am," took a long time to appear on an Etheridge album. Melissa was performing it as early as 1991, when it was part of her regular lineup. Tim Dunker says she even played a version of it in Germany in 1990. The song is about a lover who once woke Melissa in the middle of the night to tell her she was in love with someone else; it then expands on an old truism: the only sure thing is change itself.

Your Little Secret debuted on the Billboard charts at number 6, the highest of any Etheridge album. By January of 1996, it had gone platinum in the United States. This time, though, the critical reaction was mainly cool; some loved the album, but many critics — and longtime fans, as well — were unimpressed. Sales stalled for *Your Little Secret* at just over one million copies, and Etheridge confessed to a reporter that she blamed herself: she'd been too eager to put out another album. "I'm still selling as many copies of *Yes I Am* as *Your Little Secret*," she said. "I'm at that point where people are wondering which songs are on which albums" (qtd. in Deggans). Yet, according to *Q* magazine, *Your Little Secret* boasted Etheridge's "best songs to date by some distance" (Aizlewood). *Rolling Stone*, however, felt the need to do a little icon bashing: confiding that she hated to criticize Melissa because she's so likable personally, the reviewer had to say that Melissa sometimes "belts out the choruses like she's throwing them up." Furthermore, producer Hugh Padgham has a "knack for pristine bombast," and Etheridge's songs are mostly "melodramatic" and "cliché-ridden." "Shriner's Park" is all right, though (Gardner).

People agreed that "Shriner's Park" was an exception, and then went on the attack: Etheridge "needs to SHOUT TO BE HEARD!" And "Throughout much of *Your Little Secret*, Etheridge hoots and hollers like a frantic romantic who's incapable of any emotional sensation other than overcooked angst" (Helligar). *Entertainment Weekly* sneered, "Etheridge has pretty much elected herself poster girl for the local chapter of Women Who Stalk Too Much." Her "heaping portions of flame-broiled passion and want would seem to point in just one direction: the next meeting of Overstaters Anonymous" (Willman). Famous daughter Chastity Bono, undoubtedly used to seeing the media circling for the kill, provided some critical balance in the nick of time. Reviewing *Your Little Secret* for the *Advocate*, she remarked, "If *Yes I Am* was Etheridge's equivalent to Springsteen's *Born to Run*, then *Your Little Secret* may just be her *Born in the U.S.A.*" Etheridge's vocals are "gritty" and "urgent"; the album "seems to have a finger on the pulse of the nation." The only weakness

Bono identified was in some of the lyrics — these were "often repetitive and too simplistic."

Melissa herself survived this trial by media fire by hitting the road. Island Records had her busy broadening her fan base worldwide for six months following *Your Little Secret*'s release. Promotional appearances in Australia (where she opened once again for the Eagles) were followed by more in Europe. March of 1996 was spent in Canada, where Melissa rang down the curtain at the Montreal Forum. In April, Etheridge and the band returned to New Zealand, Australia, and Europe. May was reserved for some desperately needed R and R. Then they got the show back on the road again, and finally brought the whole thing home at England's mega concert venue — Wembley Stadium — on 27 July. "Her career has focused on America, and we're not totally dismayed that, outside of a few territories, Europe and the rest of the world haven't totally embraced her the way people have here," said Hooman Majd, executive VP of Island Records. "We should afford her that opportunity instead of making her pound the album home here" (qtd. in Newman, "Island Targeting Etheridge Abroad").

Fans everywhere — Melbourne, Rotterdam, Stuttgart, Ottawa, Copenhagen — embraced Melissa with their customary warmth. The *Melissa Etheridge Information Network Newsletter* was jammed with their euphoric accounts of Melissa's world-tour shows. Still, this time around Melissa had to withstand a measure of ridicule, too. Maybe it was just a manifestation of the kind of backlash overexposed superstars fall victim to, but it still seemed harsh. Reviewing a show Etheridge did at Château Lake Louise, an Alberta resort, one surly scribe misspelled her name and complained that her "image-conscious management team had such tight control over this event . . . it squeaked into a high pitch whine." She continued: "*No cameras, no* pictures, *no* drawing a likeness, *no* recording devices, *no* nothing. Sit still and be happy she's even here." The reviewer even reported seeing an unsuspecting tourist who had wandered too near the headliner being forced by Etheridge security people to eject the tape from the video camera he was carrying (Andreef). A writer for BEAT magazine (Norway's equivalent to *Rolling Stone*) also complained about how he was handled by Etheridge's management. Denied permission to take pictures, he was granted only twenty minutes of interview time. Even some of Melissa's fans joined the chorus: "management types" and "security types" had mistreated them; "some people take themselves way too seriously," they concluded.

Was *Your Little Secret* all that it should have been? Was Etheridge's management team showing a blatant disregard for the very people who supported the lifestyle to which it had become accustomed? Most of Melissa's fans didn't really care. They continued to adore her. In return, Melissa made them a gift. During her America Online chat with fans the night before she kicked off the American leg of her *Your Little Secret* tour in August of 1996, she revealed an extraordinary piece of personal news. Julie was four months pregnant. She and Melissa were going to be parents. Chatroom regulars got the news about a week before an official press release was issued. These fans respected Melissa's decision to keep other facts about the pregnancy private. They didn't ply her directly with questions that night, nor did they post them on the message board. The only postings were congratulatory notes.

Of course, after the general announcement of the pregnancy was made, a flurry of articles appeared. What was surprising, though, was the fact that the tabloids didn't run amok trying to uncover the identity of the baby's father. Etheridge had stated that the baby would know who its father was, thereby confirming that they hadn't used an anonymous sperm donor, but that appeared to be that. In any case, Julie had spoken of her own feelings about parenthood long before she became pregnant. Donor insemination, she had confided, was her and Melissa's preferred option, but "by a donor that we both knew. You see, I'm adopted, and I didn't know where I came from until I was 24, so I feel that it's important for the child to know who its biological parents are. So there'll be two mommies and Uncle Fred or Daddy whoever" ("Melissa: Rock's Great Dyke Hope"). Melissa told VH-1's *Route 96* that they thought they would name the baby Austin after Julie's favorite city in Texas (where she had attended college); early ultrasound scans had indicated that the baby would probably be a girl. The due date was announced: 25 January 1997.

However tempting it might have been for Melissa to stay at home with Julie now and prepare for motherhood in peace, the show had to go on. And go on it did. Melissa put on her trademark, high-voltage, two-and-a-half-hour show for every date on the American leg of the *Your Little Secret* tour. She exploded onto the stage with "I Really Like You," followed it up with a string of rockers, and gradually lowered the temperature with "Shriner's Park" and "Nowhere to Go." Every *Your Little Secret* track was covered — and then some: also thrown into the mix was Melissa's signature piece, "Like the Way I Do," along with "Resist," "Let Me Go," "Bring Me Some Water," and the *Yes I Am* hits. In Milwaukee, Bruce Springsteen even joined Melissa onstage for a cover of "Pink Cadillac."

For its swing through the United States, the *Your Little Secret* tour was altered in several different ways. First, former John Mellencamp drummer Kenny Aronoff came onboard, and Dave Beyer was out. Letting Dave go "was a tough decision," says Melissa, but she couldn't pass up the "opportunity to play with one of the drummers of my

MARY J. MAURO

dreams." Aronoff, as she puts it, "just takes it to another level" (qtd. in Deggans). Affectionately dubbed "the wild man" by Melissa's fans, Aronoff was able to bring a contagious energy all his own to the tour; his intense drumming imparted a primitive, jungle feel to the show's closing number, "This War Is Over." The second change involved the show's acoustic set, always performed on a small stage in the midst of the audience. This time, after the first number, the entire band would join Melissa on the little stage, where each member would be introduced to the crowd after a three-song or a four-song set. Third was the stage set. Melissa's style had always been sparse, but something new was happening here. No one was sure what to make of it. At the show's beginning, several mannequins draped in white stood on the stage; when Melissa and the band returned to the stage after the acoustic set, however, the mannequins had been disrobed, and a backdrop constructed of various disks with pictures on them had appeared. One disk was a diagram of the human eye; another, gears; another, a sonogram; another, a blue sky dotted with clouds.

Maybe the most significant alteration to the tour was the cancellation of the opening-act segment. Acts as diverse as Dishwalla, Billy Pilgrim, del Amitri, Dreams So Real, and Matthew Sweet had warmed up the crowds for Melissa in the past. No more. The decision came as a bit of a surprise to fans. Like clockwork, the *Your Little Secret* show would begin at 8:00 and the party would break up as early as 10:30. It was now plugged as an "Evening with Melissa Etheridge." Nobody seemed put out that the evenings ended early, though — particularly because, during some of the concerts, Melissa would have an extra burst of energy and play for as long as three hours.

Melissa performs during the Your Little Secret *tour*
DANIELLE BRADLEY

Melissa was maintaining quality control: her shows were, as ever, of the first order. Still, fans posting online reviews would occasionally remark that she looked a bit tired. Finally, in October of 1996, during the second leg of the American tour, Melissa confessed that she was finding it very difficult to tour while Julie remained at home pregnant and alone. "It's so tough," she sighed. "We were a little over-optimistic in planning this thing." Their thinking had been that the tour would end in December, and that Melissa would at least be around for that crucial ninth month. But it wasn't as easy as it sounded: "I call Julie and she says, 'I'm hungry,' and I wish I could go get her something to eat. It gets harder as the pregnancy progresses. Julie came out on a recent leg of the tour and hung around New York for a while. We hung out in Chicago. She'll come out and that makes it better, but it is so hard to wake up every morning and not be able to touch her belly." Next time, she continued, "I'll plan it better. And I'll certainly be sticking close to home after the baby comes. I've been a road hound for eight years and that's going to change" ("Anthem-Belting Etheridge").

That change could take some tantalizing forms. Hollywood beckons. A whole new career path is opening up for Melissa that will bring her in off the road for extended periods and (most of the time) keep her close to home and hearth — *and* keep her visible to her ardent fans. Though her publicist and manager presently deny that the deal is set, Melissa has been chosen to play Janis Joplin in Marc Rocco's upcoming biopic, scheduled to start shooting in February of 1997. It's a far cry from her amateur theater days — when she tackled the roles of Aunt Eller in *Oklahoma* and Dorothy in the *Wizard of Oz* — but Melissa has embraced the opportunity of portraying her anguished rock heroine on the big screen with relish. According to Rocco (whose previous directing credits include *Murder in* the First and Where the Day Takes You; he also coproduced Teresa's Tattoo for Julie), an acting coach was hired to accompany Melissa on the Your Little Secret tour. "Her progress has been substantial," Rocco continues. "I'm completely convinced she can do this, and I think it will be like Diana Ross in Lady Sings the Blues" (qtd. in Fleming). Julie actually wrote the original script for the movie, and Rocco has revised it.

Preliminary work on packaging the film has been fraught with difficulties. A competing TriStar biopic is currently in production and has been authorized by the Joplin family. It stars Joplin look-alike Lili Taylor and director Nancy Savoca has penned the script, which is based on Laura Joplin's 1992 biography of her sister, who died in 1970. Laura Joplin is "aggressively opposed" to Rocco's project. "He has nothing except the ability to do a public domain piece," she points out. "He's licensed some music, but has nothing exclusive. And there are 23 songs or so we control" (qtd. in Sandler).

In the Savoca film, Taylor will lip-synch to Joplin recordings. In Rocco's unauthorized version, Etheridge will — of course! — belt out the songs herself. Her aim is to re-create Joplin, not imitate her. She will have to limit herself to songs that are not owned by the Joplin family, and this will present a challenge. The Rocco-Etheridge team does have one ace up its sleeve, though: it has the support of Big Brother and the Holding Company, Joplin's legendary band. On 2 June 1996, Etheridge joined Big Brother onstage at San Francisco's Maritime Theater for a three-song "audition" set that included "Down on Me," "Ball and Chain," and "Piece of My Heart." It's fortuitous that this last tune, a perennial Etheridge favorite, is one of the songs Etheridge and Rocco are allowed to use in the film. In the audience that night was Cassandra Berns, daughter of the late Bert Berns, one of the song's co-writers; she saw for herself that Melissa's rendition of "Piece of My Heart" did justice to her father's work. Big Brothers Sam Andrew and James Gurley (both on guitar), Peter Albin (on bass), and David Getz (on drums) were favorably impressed with Melissa's tribute to Janis, and on the strength of this impression pledged their cooperation. "She sure pulled off 'Ball and Chain,' " remarked Andrew (qtd. in Selvin). Getz agreed: "She was believable in capturing the spirit" (qtd. in Gerhard). Now it's full steam ahead: Paramount is slated to distribute the biopic in the United States, and rumor has it that screen heartthrob and talented actor Brad Pitt will play the role of Kris Kristofferson.

And after the Joplin film is in the can? One thing is certain: Melissa will continue to write and perform music — it's in her blood and has been since she was a child. But, she says, "I think I have finished the phase of my writing that was very relationship-oriented and broken-heart-oriented. That's obviously not what I'm going through right now." Instead, she's "moving out from introspective, emotional songwriting . . . to an outward, worldly sort of feeling." She adds that, with a child on the way, "You become more concerned, and you really do want to make the world a better place. It sounds corny, but you do" (qtd. in Lustig).

It's possible that political activism, long a vital part of Etheridge's public life, will move to the forefront of her art. Her rage against inequity, her empathy with the human victims of ruthless ideological struggles, could provide her music with the edge and the angst that unstable relationships once did. Etheridge's personal life is at last a model of stability. She and Julie have been together for eight years now. Recently, Melissa has announced that they'd like to have "three or four or five more children" (Mark Miller). In anticipation of parenthood, they've relocated to a more secluded home and taken their menagerie with them: two cats, Gwendolyn and Gabrielle (named after Anne Rice's *Interview with the Vampire* character); two dogs, Angel and Bingo; and a cockatoo named Boo that bobs its head and dances whenever someone whistles the theme from the old *Leave It to Beaver* show. Gold and platinum records adorn Melissa and Julie's walls, as do the works of ten-year-old Romanian prodigy Alexandra Nechita. The couple has made it onto Hollywood's A-list: their friends include Bruce Springsteen and wife Patty Scialfa, Laura Dern, Jeff Goldblum, Ellen DeGeneres, Rosie O'Donnell, Brad Pitt, and k.d. lang. When Melissa wanted to become a vegetarian, k.d. actually moved in with her and Julie for a week or so to give them a crash course in meatless cooking. (Melissa, for health reasons, eventually decided to allow a little fish and poultry back into her diet.)

Like most superstars, especially those with families, Melissa strives to live a normal life. She and Julie don't go out to clubs much; they prefer to have dinner with friends. They've also been known to indulge in the odd game of swimming-pool basketball — in the middle of the night. When their energy flags, Melissa and Julie like to veg out together in front of the tube; *America's Funniest Home Videos* is one favorite stress reliever. "When I come home from the road it is so great to feel routine," Melissa says. "Julie and I each take care of certain things around the house. I feed the dog in the morning." The two also retreat to their cabin in the San Bernardino Mountains, ski, and snorkel ("Forever Etheridge").

"She really is appealingly corny," said *Rolling Stone*'s Jancee Dunn of Melissa after interviewing her for that magazine in 1995. "She took me up to her little office upstairs in her house and there was a little cat in the office. The cat climbed onto my lap and Melissa showed me trophies and stuff that she has received. One of them she received from her hometown for 'Melissa Etheridge Day.' When she was showing it to me she was getting a little choked up. She showed me a picture of her Grandma which was hanging on the wall who, by the way, looks exactly like her and she got a little choked up then, too. It was just nice to see someone who was so genuinely appreciative of everything" ("*Rolling Stone*'s Jancee Dunn").

Though Melissa readily admits that she's got an ego just like everybody else, the humility that Dunn describes is fundamental to her nature. It is most likely born of the spirituality that has always remained a part of her life. Although she rejected organized religion long ago, Melissa still asserts that her deepest values come "from recognizing intolerance, in myself and in others. The philosophy I follow is that I am one with everyone else." This philosophy derives from Buddhism and Taoism: "I'm not a follower of these religions," Melissa says, but "I can't look at anyone and say, 'They aren't a part of me.' They are" ("Forever Etheridge").

All of this is linked to the huge appeal Etheridge holds for the legions of fans who flock to her shows: they are inspired by her music, her activism, her life, and her very self. "She is loud and explosive," says fan Janinne Meloni. She is "soft and tender, she is in your face, yet she'll hold your hand. She's fiery, passionate, sweet and soulful, and let us not forget, she's human." But perhaps Tim Dunker, the German Superfan, says it best: "Melissa, I am simply thankful for your music. It gives me a power and strength I can't describe. I am also thankful for the way you are. Stay the person you are, become a great mother, speak true, and please, please, keep on rocking!"

DISCOGRAPHY

From the discography compiled by members of the
Melissa Etheridge Internet Mailing List and Online Fan Club
(http://www.ecw.ca/mle).

Track listings are only included for items with nonalbum tracks.

ALBUMS

Melissa Etheridge (1988)

1.	Similar Features	[4:42]
2.	Chrome Plated Heart	[3:59]
3.	Like the Way I Do	[5:23]
4.	Precious Pain	[4:15]
5.	Don't You Need	[4:59]
6.	The Late September Dogs	[6:33]
7.	Occasionally	[2:36]
8.	Watching You	[5:33]
9.	Bring Me Some Water	[3:52]
10.	I Want You	[4:07]

Brave and Crazy (1989)

1.	No Souvenirs	[4:33]
2.	Brave and Crazy	[4:37]
3.	You Used to Love to Dance	[4:33]
4.	The Angels	[4:38]
5.	You Can Sleep while I Drive	[3:14]
6.	Testify	[4:28]
7.	Let Me Go	[3:56]
8.	My Back Door	[4:24]
9.	Skin Deep	[3:10]
10.	Royal Station 4/16	[6:40]

Never Enough (1992)

1.	Ain't It Heavy	[4:20]
2.	2001	[4:36]
3.	Dance without Sleeping	[5:40]
4.	Place Your Hand	[3:24]
5.	Must Be Crazy for Me	[3:43]
6.	Meet Me in the Back	[4:02]
7.	The Boy Feels Strange	[4:31]
8.	Keep It Precious	[6:13]
9.	The Letting Go	[3:05]
10.	It's for You	[5:41]

Yes I Am (1993)

1.	I'm the Only One	[4:54]
2.	If I Wanted To	[3:55]
3.	Come to My Window	[3:55]
4.	Silent Legacy	[5:22]
5.	I Will Never Be the Same	[4:41]
6.	All American Girl	[4:05]
7.	Yes I Am	[4:24]
8.	Resist	[2:57]
9.	Ruins	[4:53]
10.	Talking to My Angel	[4:48]

Your Little Secret (1995)

1.	Your Little Secret	[4:19]
2.	I Really Like You	[4:09]
3.	Nowhere to Go	[5:53]
4.	An Unusual Kiss	[5:21]
5.	I Want to Come Over	[5:25]
6.	All the Way to Heaven	[4:54]
7.	I Could Have Been You	[5:56]
8.	Shriner's Park	[5:23]
9.	Change	[4:37]
10.	This War Is Over	[6:57]

MINI-ALBUMS

U.S. PROMOTIONAL SINGLE CD RELEASE

Melissa Etheridge — Live (1988)

1.	Chrome Plated Heart (live)	[3:36]
2.	The Late September Dogs (live)	[6:35]
3.	Similar Features (live)	[4:36]
4.	Bring Me Some Water (live)	[4:24]
5.	Like the Way I Do (live)	[10:13]

(All tracks recorded live on 11 October 1988 at the Roxy, Hollywood, CA. Tracks 1, 3, 4, and 5 were also released as a German commercial single CD in 1988.)

U.S. PROMOTIONAL SINGLE CD RELEASE

Melissa Etheridge — Live (1990)

1.	Skin Deep (live)	[3:46]
2.	Royal Station 4/16 (live)	[11:06]
3.	You Can Sleep while I Drive (live)	[3:37]
4.	Let Me Go (live)	[8:00]

(All tracks recorded live on 20 October 1989.)

U.K. PROMOTIONAL SINGLE CD RELEASE

Melissa Etheridge — Live (1992)

1.	Bring Me Some Water (live)	[4:22]
2.	Let Me Go (live)	[7:31]
3.	Skin Deep (live)	[3:42]
4.	Like the Way I Do (live)	[10:13]

(This disk was a free promotional CD available with initial copies of *Never Enough* from HMV Records in the U.K.)

Melissa Etheridge — The Basement Tapes (1993)

1.	Come to My Window (live)	[3:58]
2.	The Letting Go (live)	[3:35]
3.	No Souvenirs (live)	[4:58]
4.	Bring Me Some Water (live)	[4:13]

(All tracks are live acoustic solo performances. This disk was a bonus included with some Australian editions of *Yes I Am*. The CD itself doesn't have a date on it.)

COMMERCIAL SINGLE CD RELEASE

Melissa Etheridge — Live (1995)

1.	Come to My Window (live)	[4:01]
2.	No Souvenirs (live)	[5:00]
3.	Ain't It Heavy (live)	[4:20]
4.	Yes I Am (live)	[4:23]

(This is a live CD that came as an extra with some of the first few [limited edition] copies worldwide of *Your Little Secret*. Tracks 1 and 3 were recorded in 1994. Track 1 is the same as on the ''All American Girl'' single.)

SIMILAR FEATURES

COMMERCIAL RELEASE

Similar Features (1988)

COMMERCIAL 7" VINYL SINGLE RELEASE

Similar Features (1988)

1.	Similar Features (edit)	[3:55]
2.	Bring Me Some Water (live)	[4:22]

U.S. PROMOTIONAL 12" VINYL SINGLE RELEASE

Similar Features (1988)

A.	Similar Features (vocal edit)	[3:55]
B.	Similar Features (album version)	[4:22]

BRING ME SOME WATER

COMMERCIAL RELEASE

Bring Me Some Water (1988)

DUTCH COMMERCIAL CD RELEASE

2 Meter Sessies Volume 1 (1991)

1.	Bring Me Some Water (acoustic)	[3:40]

(This is a live acoustic performance on a Dutch radio show, recorded in May of 1988. The CD has a total of 18 acoustic tracks.)

U.S. COMMERCIAL CD RELEASE

Grammy's Greatest Moments — Volume IV (1994)

    11.   Bring Me Some Water   [3:59]

(Performed on 22 February 1989.)

LIKE THE WAY I DO

COMMERCIAL RELEASE

Like the Way I Do (1988)

COMMERCIAL 7″ VINYL SINGLE RELEASE

Like the Way I Do (1988)

    A.   Like the Way I Do
    B.   Bring Me Some Water (live)

AUSTRALIAN 7″ VINYL SINGLE RELEASE

Like the Way I Do (1988)

    A.   Like the Way I Do (edit)
    B.   Chrome Plated Heart (live)

(Track B was recorded live on 11 October 1988 at the Roxy, Hollywood, CA. This is a limited-edition release.)

COMMERCIAL CD RELEASE

The Greatest Hits '93 — Volume 1 (1993)

    12.   Like the Way I Do (live)   [10:10]

(Recorded live on 11 October 1988 at the Roxy, Hollywood, CA. "Like the Way I Do" [live] was rereleased in the Netherlands and became a hit for the second time. This track was also available on a Dutch commercial 2-CD release: "Het Beste Uit De Mega Top 50 Van '93" [1993], and a sampler: "If This Were a Radio It Would Sound Like the Future" [1989].)

D
I
S
C
O
G
R
A
P
H
Y

CHROME PLATED HEART

COMMERCIAL RELEASE

Chrome Plated Heart (1988)

U.S. PROMOTIONAL SINGLE CD RELEASE

Chrome Plated Heart (1988)

| 1. | Chrome Plated Heart | [3:59] |
| 2. | Chrome Plated Heart (live) | [3:36] |

DON'T YOU NEED

U.K. COMMERCIAL SINGLE CD RELEASE

Don't You Need (1988)

1.	Don't You Need (edit)	[3:54]
2.	Similar Features (acoustic)	[4:05]
3.	Precious Pain (acoustic)	[3:51]
4.	Don't You Need (acoustic)	[4:20]

NO SOUVENIRS

U.K. COMMERCIAL SINGLE CD RELEASE

No Souvenirs (1989)

1.	No Souvenirs	[4:33]
2.	Brave and Crazy (live)	[4:37]
3.	No Souvenirs (live)	[4:43]

(Track 2 actually plays for 5:37. Live tracks recorded live at the Paramount Theater, Denver, Colorado. Tracks 1 and 3 [and sometimes track 2] were also included in various versions of this release worldwide.)

U.S. COMMERCIAL CD RELEASE

ONXRT: *Live from the Archives Volume 1* (1993)

1.   No Souvenirs

(Release date: 16 November 1993)

(Recorded live at the Park West, 13 October 1989. Released in the WXRT listening area only, and only in CD form. This CD contains 14 tracks in total.)

THE ANGELS

COMMERCIAL SINGLE CD RELEASE

The Angels (1989)

1.   The Angels (alternate studio version) [4:04]
2.   The Angels (live)   [4:44]
3.   Chrome Plated Heart (live)   [4:20]

(Live tracks recorded at the Bottom Line, New York City.)

LET ME GO

U.S. COMMERCIAL SINGLE CD RELEASE

Let Me Go (1989)

1.   Let Me Go   [3:56]
2.   Let Me Go (live)   [8:00]
3.   Occasionally (live)   [3:20]

COMMERCIAL SINGLE RELEASE

You Can Sleep while I Drive (1989)

1.	You Can Sleep while I Drive	[3:14]
2.	You Can Sleep while I Drive (live)	[3:37]
3.	The Late September Dogs (live)	[6:33]

AIN'T IT HEAVY

COMMERCIAL SINGLE CD RELEASE

Ain't It Heavy (1992)

1.	Ain't It Heavy	[4:20]
2.	The Boy Feels Strange	[4:31]
3.	Royal Station 4/16 (live)	[11:06]

(Track 3 was recorded on 20 October 1989.)

2001

COMMERCIAL SINGLE RELEASE

2001 (1992)

1.	2001	[4:36]
2.	Meet Me in the Back (live)	[4:48]
3.	Testify (live)	[4:39]

(Track 2 is from the Album Network.)

2001 (1992)

1.	2001 (remix)	[4:12]
2.	2001 (album)	[4:36]
3.	2001 (12" remix)	[8:01]
4.	Meet Me in the Back (live)	[4:48]

(Track 4 is from the Album Network.)

U.S. PROMOTIONAL VINYL RELEASE

2001 (1992)

A.   Melissa Etheridge — 2001 (LP version) [4:36]
Eh?   Vic Reeves — Dizzy (coffee-break mix) [4:32]

(This one's kind of unusual, in that it has Melissa on one side and Vic Reeves on the other. It really does say Side A and Side Eh? [a Canadian expression]. It has a bright-orange plain cardboard sleeve.)

DANCE WITHOUT SLEEPING

COMMERCIAL SINGLE CD RELEASE

Dance without Sleeping (1992)

1.	Dance without Sleeping (edit)	[4:13]
2.	Similar Features (live)	[4:42]
3.	Ain't It Heavy (live)	[5:33]

(Track 2 was recorded live on 11 October 1988 at the Roxy, Hollywood, CA. Track 3 is from *Live at the Record Plant*.)

GERMAN COMMERCIAL SINGLE CD RELEASE

Must Be Crazy for Me (1993)

1.   Must Be Crazy for Me   [3:43]
2.   Must Be Crazy for Me (live)   [5:07]
3.   Keep It Precious (live)   [9:57]

(This CD was released in the Netherlands only.)

I'M THE ONLY ONE

U.S. COMMERCIAL SINGLE CD RELEASE

I'm the Only One (1994)

1.   I'm the Only One (album version)   [4:54]
2.   Maggie May (live)   [6:18]
3.   Ain't It Heavy (live)   [4:13]
4.   I'm the Only One (live)   [5:26]

(Track 2 was recorded on 10 March 1994 in Montreal. Track 3 is a live solo acoustic version, probably recorded on 10 March 1994. Track 4 is live from 1994, probably recorded 10 March. Definitely not the version on the U.K. release.)

U.K. COMMERCIAL SINGLE CD RELEASE

I'm the Only One (1993)

1.   I'm the Only One (edit)   [4:15]
2.   Bring Me Some Water (live)   [4:22]
3.   I'm the Only One (live)   [5:30]
4.   Yes I Am (live)   [5:02]

(Track 2 was recorded live on 11 October 1988 at the Roxy, Hollywood, CA. Track 3 is probably from a show from the summer of 1993, unlike the U.S. edition with the live version from 1994.)

COME TO MY WINDOW

COMMERCIAL SINGLE CD RELEASE

Come to My Window (1993)

1.	Come to My Window	[3:55]
2.	Ain't It Heavy (live)	[5:34]
3.	The Letting Go (live)	[3:51]
4.	I'm the Only One (live)	[5:30]

(Track 2 is from the *Record Plant*, 1992.)

U.S. PROMOTIONAL SINGLE CD RELEASE

Come to My Window (1993)

1.	Come to My Window (a/c mix)	[3:56]
2.	Come to My Window (lite mix)	[3:56]
3.	Come to My Window (edit)	[3:34]
4.	Come to My Window (album version)	[3:55]

U.S. PROMOTIONAL CD RELEASE

Cream of Cuts with Fresh Sounds (1995)

Come to My Window (live)	[3:26]

(This is a live solo acoustic version, recorded in 1993 at KBCO Studio C, Boulder, CO. The CD has a total of 18 tracks. Also available on: *Tune Up* [rock], vol. 110, from the week of 24 January 1994.)

ALL AMERICAN GIRL

GERMAN COMMERCIAL SINGLE CD RELEASE

All American Girl (1994)

1.	All American Girl	[4:05]
2.	Come to My Window (live)	[4:02]
3.	All American Girl (live)	[4:32]

Tune Up 114 (Rock, for 18 April 1994) (1994)

13.	All American Girl (live)	[4:33]

(This track was recorded for the Album Network's broadcast in Montreal. This sampler has a total of 15 tracks.)

IF I WANTED TO

U.S. COMMERCIAL SINGLE CD RELEASE

If I Wanted To (1994)

1.	If I Wanted To	[3:55]
2.	Maggie May (live)	[6:18]
3.	I'm the Only One (live)	[5:26]

U.S. COMMERCIAL SINGLE CD RELEASE

If I Wanted To (1995)

1.	If I Wanted To	[3:29]
2.	Come to My Window (live)	[3:21]
3.	Bring Me Some Water (live)	[4:35]
4.	Like the Way I Do (livc)	[10:12]

(Tracks 3 and 4 were recorded live on 11 October 1988 at the Roxy, Hollywood, CA.)

YES I AM

SAMPLER

The Cities' Sampler Vol. 5: Rarities

2.	Yes I Am (live)	[4:51]

(This sampler is put out by the Minneapolis-based radio station KTCZ 97.1, which calls itself "The Cities' 97.")

On the Mountain (1994)

Yes I Am (live) [3:30]

(This track was recorded on 22 September 1993. This CD is put out by a radio station based in Seattle, and recorded on behalf of the Wilderness Society.)

HAPPY XMAS (WAR IS OVER)

U.S. PROMOTIONAL SINGLE CD RELEASE

Happy Xmas (War Is Over/Give Peace a Chance) (1994)

1. Happy Xmas (War Is Over/
Give Peace a Chance) [4:36]

YOUR LITTLE SECRET

COMMERCIAL SINGLE CD RELEASE

Your Little Secret (1995)

1. Your Little Secret (LP version) [4:20]
2. All American Girl (live) [4:29]
3. Bring Me Some Water (live) [4:18]
4. Skin Deep (live) [3:45]

(Track 3 was recorded in 1988.)

Your Little Secret (1995)

1.	Your Little Secret (album version)	[4:19]
2.	All American Girl (live)	[4:29]
3.	Chrome Plated Heart (live)	[3:33]
4.	Keep It Precious (live)	[8:56]

(Track 3 was recorded in 1988. Track 4 was recorded in 1993.)

I WANT TO COME OVER

U.S. COMMERCIAL SINGLE RELEASE

I Want to Come Over (1996)

NOWHERE TO GO

COMMERCIAL SINGLE CD RELEASE

Nowhere to Go (1996)

1.	Nowhere to Go (remix)	[4:15]
2.	Bring Me Some Water (live, with Joan Osborne)	[5:15]
3.	Nowhere to Go (live)	[5:03]

(The Australian Commercial Single CD Release includes an additional track, Like the Way I Do [10:14].)

Melissa and Joan Osborne
From VH-1 Duets, *Doheny Mansion, L.A.*
NEAL PRESTON/RETNA

MISCELLANEOUS

U.S. PROMOTIONAL RELEASE

Never Enough Box Set

(Contains video, audio tape [5 songs], and press booklet.)

CANADIAN PROMOTIONAL RELEASE

Melissa Etheridge (Never Enough Interview) (1992)

(Global Satellite Network interview; CD includes cue sheet, as only the answers are on the CD.)

Weeds (soundtrack) (1987)

I Wanna Go Home   [1:46]

(This track was written by Melissa Etheridge.)

SAMPLER

For Our Children

7.   The Green Grass Grew all Around

U.S. COMMERCIAL RELEASE

It's Now or Never: The Elvis Tribute (1994)

5.   Burning Love   [3:04]

U.S. COMMERCIAL RELEASE

Boys on the Side (soundtrack) (1995)

2.   I Take You with Me   [4:48]

(Contains a total of 13 tracks.)

U.S. COMMERCIAL RELEASE

Ain't Nuthin' But a She Thing (1995)

4.   The Weakness in Me

(This is a charity album benefiting the Shirley Divers Foundation, named after a former Sire A & R executive who died from breast cancer in 1992. Various other artists also appear in duets with, or covering, other artists. On this track Melissa covers Joan Armatrading.)

U.S. COMMERCIAL RELEASE

Don Henley, *The End of the Innocence* (1989)

8.   Gimme What You Got

(Melissa Etheridge sings backup vocals.)

U.S. COMMERCIAL RELEASE

Holly Near, *Singer in the Storm* (1990)

Singer in the Storm

(Guitar track by Melissa Etheridge. The CD book simply lists Melissa as one of the players on the album, but does not list individual credits on the songs. In the promotional video for the album, Holly mentions that Melissa recorded the guitar track for the title song. The album is a live concert with extra tracks [vocal and instrumental] added afterwards in the studio.)

U.S. COMMERCIAL RELEASE

Delbert McClinton, *Never Been Rocked Enough* (1992)

1.   Everytime I Roll the Dice
2.   Can I Change My Mind

(Background vocals by Melissa Etheridge on both tracks.)

COMMERCIAL SINGLE CD RELEASE

Bryan Adams, *Star* (1996)

3.   It's Only Love (live)

(Recorded live at Wembley Stadium on 27 July 1996, with Melissa Etheridge.)

WORKS CONSULTED

Aizlewood, John. "Oranges Are Not the Only Fruit." *Q* Jan. 1996: 76–78.

Albertsen, Lorna. E-mail to the author. 30 June 1996.

Anderson, Diane. "Melissa as You've Never Seen Her." *Girlfriends* Jan.–Feb. 1996: 6–9.

Andreef, Monica. "Etheridge's Music Great but Security Was Excessive." *Bow Valley This Week* 19 Mar. 1996: 5.

"Are You Man Enough?" *Advocate* 1 Nov. 1994: 79.

Arnold, Sue. "Leaving Him for Her." *New Weekly* 1 Apr. 1996: 30–33.

Banaszak, Taylor. E-mail to the author. 18 Jan. 1996.

Baumgardner, Ed. "Long Journey." *Winston-Salem Journal* 18 Nov. 1994.

Beebe, Barbara. "Powerful, Eloquent — Yes, She Is." *Record Exchange Music Monitor* Jan. 1995: 1.

Bergquist, Kathie. "Yes, I Am." *Outlines* Nov. 1993.

Bono, Chastity. "Honky-Tonk Woman." *Advocate* 14 Nov. 1995: 97–98.

Britt, Bruce. "Etheridge Shows Softer Side." *Los Angeles Daily News* 3 Sept. 1992.

——. "Etheridge Softens Her Style in Los Angeles Concert." *Santa Cruz Sentinel* 4 Sept. 1992: 11.

Brown, Dana. Telephone interview. 7 May 1996.

Browne, David. "Melissa Etheridge Does a Phony Joni." *New York Daily News* 28 Sept. 1989.

Carswell, Sue. "Thoroughly Modern Melissa." *Out* Dec.–Jan. 1994: 81–85.

Castro, Peter, and John Griffiths. "A House in Harmony." *People Weekly* 5 Sept. 1994: 57–58.

Clair, Kim. Telephone interview. 6 Feb. 1996.

Cohen, Rich. "Adult Videos: VH-1 Gambles Its Future on a New Generation of Stars." *Us* July 1995: 73–78, 93.

Cullen, Jim. "Never Enough." *Rolling Stone* 14 May 1992: 103.

Deggans, Eric. "Everywhere to Go." *St. Petersburg Times* 1 Nov. 1996: 20–21.

Dietrich, Briana. E-mail to the author. 24 Jan. 1996.

Dobkin, Alix. Letter to the author. 23 Feb. 1996.

——. Telephone interview. 16 Mar. 1996.

Drier, Dawn, and Michelle Keller. Interview with Dawn Soldan. 8 June 1996.

Dunker, Tim. E-mail to the author. 24 Aug. 1996.

——. E-mail to the author. 31 Aug. 1996.

——. E-mail to the author. 29 Sept. 1996.

Dunn, Jancee. "Melissa Etheridge Takes the Long Hard Road from the Heartland to Hollywood." *Rolling Stone* 1 June 1995: 38–45.

——. "*Rolling Stone*'s Jancee Dunn Takes MEIN behind the Scenes." *Melissa Etheridge Information Network Newsletter* 2.1.

Edie, Paul. Telephone interview. 1 July 1996.

Elkins, Elizabeth. E-mail to the author. 15 Apr. 1996.

Etheridge, Melissa. "Anthem-Belting Etheridge, Soon to Be Parent, Looks Forward to Calmer Schedule." With Paul Hampel. *St. Louis Post-Dispatch* 4 Oct. 1996.

——. "Forever Etheridge." With Maureen Littlejohn. *Modern Woman* Apr. 1996.

——. "A Fresh Out Look: Melissa Etheridge's Coming Out Hasn't Stopped Her from Being In." With Lydia Carole DeFretos. *BAM* 3 Dec. 1993: 46+.

——. "How I Wrote That Hit Song." *Musician* Jan.–Feb. 1995: 13.

——. "It's Melissa: I Had to Post." *America Online*. Online posting. Melissa Etheridge Board, Music Message Center. 2 Apr. 1996.

——. "Kansas Girl Paid Rock and Roll Dues." With C.J. Janovy. *Note* Dec. 1992: 8–9.

——. "Melissa Etheridge." *San Jose Mercury News* 14 Aug. 1994.

——. "Melissa Etheridge." With Fred Schruers. *Us* Dec. 1995: 98–102.

——. "Melissa Etheridge: In through the Out Door." With Rich Cohen. *Rolling Stone* 29 Dec. 1994–12 Jan. 1995: 110+.

——. "Melissa Etheridge: The Interview." With Jane Kansas. *Wayves* Apr. 1996: 2–3.

———. "Melissa Etheridge: LN's Exclusive Interview." With Karen Ocamb. *Lesbian News* Sept. 1993: 40–41, 60–61, 65.

———. "Melissa Etheridge: Rocking the Boat." *Advocate* 21 Sept. 1993: 50–53.

———. "Melissa Etheridge: The Set Yourself Free Revolution." With Ingrid Casares. *Interview* Oct. 1994: 168+.

———. "Melissa Etheridge: She's Not in Kansas Anymore." With C.J. Janovy. *10 Percent* Mar.–Apr. 1994: 54–57, 76.

———. "Melissa Still on the Road." *Melissa Etheridge Information Network Newsletter* 1.3.

———. "The Only One: Melissa Etheridge." Unpublished interview. With Diane Bailey. 22 Nov. 1993.

———. "Person of the Year: Melissa Etheridge." With Judy Wieder. *Advocate* 23 Jan. 1996: 64–73.

———. "Yes, She Is: Melissa Etheridge." With Toni Armstrong. *Hot Wire* Jan. 1994: 2–5, 60.

———. "Yes, She Is . . . Talking with Melissa Etheridge." With Surina Khan. *Metroline* 3 Mar. 1994.

———, and Julie Cypher. "Melissa: Rock's Great Dyke Hope." With Judy Wieder. *Advocate* 26 July 1994: 45–56.

Everett, Todd. "Not in Kansas Anymore . . ." *BAM* 3 Dec. 1993: 47, 50, 82.

Finaly, Liza. Untitled. *Impact* Nov. 1993: 6.

Findlay, Heather. "Teresa's Tattoo." *Girlfriends* May–June 1995: 31.

Fleming, Michael. "Janis Joplin Projects Compete for Piece of Box Office." *Reuters News Service Online*. Online posting. 30 Sept. 1996.

Folsom, Steve. "Making Melissa Sound Great: An Interview with Steve Folsom." *Melissa Etheridge Information Network Newsletter* 2.4.

Frankel, Martha. "No Diamond in the Rough." *Movieline* Aug. 1996: 56–61.

Gardner, Elysa. "Your Little Secret." *Rolling Stone* 30 Nov. 1995: 68.

Gaar, Gillian. *She's a Rebel: The History of Women in Rock and Roll*. Seattle: Seal, 1992.

Gerhard, Susan. "Saving the World: Big Brother-ly Love." *San Francisco Bay Guardian* 3–9 July 1996: 40.

Giardina, Kim. Personal interview. 15 Aug. 1996.

Givens, Ron. "Melissa Etheridge." *Stereo Review* Jan. 1990: 112.

Helligar, Jeremy. "Your Little Secret." *People Weekly* 20 Nov. 1995: 23.

Hicks, Shannon. "Etheridge's Passion Fills New Haven Coliseum." *Newtown Bee* 16 Dec. 1994.

Hunt, Dennis. "Is Melissa Etheridge the Doom-and-Gloom Star of Rock?" *Los Angeles Times* 17 Oct. 1989: F6.

Johnson, David. E-mail to the author. 21 Feb. 1996.

Johnson, Peter. E-mail to the author. 8 Mar. 1996.

Katz, Larry. "For the Record: Pop's 4 Unspun Heroines." *Boston Herald* 14 Apr. 1989.

Kennedy, Dana. "The Unplugged Melissa Etheridge." *Entertainment Weekly* 17 Mar. 1995: 42–45.

Kirk, Kris. "Jealous Guise." *Melody Maker* 28 May 1988: 38.

Loza, Gabriela. Telephone interview. 10 Feb. 1996.

Lustig, Jay. "Melissa Etheridge: Impending Parenthood Leads to a Change in Attitude." *Internet*. Online posting. Melissa Etheridge Mailing List. 28 Aug. 1996.

Maples, Tina. "Passionate Etheridge and New Band Put on Rousing Show before 3,000." *Milwaukee Journal* 25 Apr. 1994.

Mason, Rick. "Eschewing the Electric." *St. Paul Pioneer Press-Dispatch* 16 Mar. 1989.

Mathur, Paul. "Live." *Melody Maker* 4 June 1988: 19.

McCrea, Kathleen. E-mail to the author. 29 Jan. 1996.

McTavish, Brian. "Etheridge Braves New Style." *Kansas City Star* 4 Dec. 1992.

Meloni, Janinne. Letter to the author. 5 May 1996.

Miller, John. E-mail to the author. 8 July 1996.

Miller, Mark. "We're a Family and We Have Rights." *Newsweek* 4 Nov. 1996: 54–55.

Milward, John. "A Personal Touch." *Newsday* 24 Sept. 1989.

Mohn, Tristan. "There's No Place like Home." *Leavenworth Times* 13 Nov. 1994.

Morden, Darryl. Rev. of *Never Enough*. CD *Review* June 1992.

Morse, Steve. "Melissa Etheridge Comes into Her Own." *Boston Globe*. Newsbank. Online. 2 Dec. 1996.

Nash, Alanna. "Melissa Etheridge: Never Enough." *Stereo Review* June 1992: 85–86.

——— . "Woodstock '94." *Stereo Review* Feb. 1995: 142–43.

Nelson, Jim. "Melissa Etheridge." *Album Network* 3 Nov. 1995: 24–25.

Newman, Melinda. "Island Targeting Etheridge Abroad." *Billboard* 14 Oct. 1995: 1, 92.

——— . "Talent in Action: Melissa Etheridge." *Billboard* 11 Nov. 1989: 36.

Novak, Ralph. "Brave and Crazy." *People Weekly* 13 Nov. 1989: 25.

——— . "Melissa Etheridge." *People Weekly* 8 Aug. 1988: 24.

——— . "Never Enough." *People Weekly* 4 May 1992: 21.

"Ode to Etheridge's Courage of Convictions." *San Jose Mercury News* 21 July 1994.

Outerbridge, Laura. "Melissa Etheridge: Songs of Love Gone Wrong." *Washington Times* 1 May 1989: E3.

Padgham, Hugh. "Hugh Padgham Interview." *Melissa Etheridge Information Network Newsletter* 2.2.

Passarelli, Lauren, and Cindy Brown. Personal interview with Kim Giardina. 3 Apr. 1996.

Payne, Mona Shield, and Elizabeth Handy. *America Online*. Online posting. Melissa Etheridge Board, Music Message Center. 25 Jan. 1996.

Phoenix, Val. "Melissa Etheridge: Yes, She Is." *Deneuve* Dec. 1993: 28+.

Puterbaugh, Parke. "Melissa Etheridge: Yes I Am." *Stereo Review* Jan. 1994: 126.

Ramos, David, and Richard Ramos. Telephone interview. 12 Feb. 1996.

Ransom, Kevin. "Melissa Etheridge: With a Bullet." *CD Review* June 1995: 25–26.

Resnicoff, Matt. "Braving the Acoustic Craze." *Guitar Player* Nov. 1989: 10–11.

"Rocker Melissa Etheridge, Who Is Both Acoustic and Electrifying." *People Weekly* 15 May 1989: 183.

Rodgers, Jeffrey Pepper. "Gearbox: Melissa Etheridge." *Acoustic Guitar* Mar. 1996: 83.

——— . "Unleashed." *Acoustic Guitar* Mar. 1996: 54–63.

Rogovoy, Seth. "Melissa Etheridge Finds Joy in Her Audience." *Berkshire Eagle* 29 July 1990.

Romero, Cathy. Telephone interview. 26 Feb. 1996.

Rotenstein, David. *America Online*. Online posting. Melissa Etheridge Board, Music Message Center. 7 Mar. 1996.

Ruhlmann, William. "Melissa Etheridge's Long Road to Stardom." *New York Tribune* 6 Oct. 1989.

Russell, Deborah. "Etheridge Promotes AIDS Awareness: 'Girl' Vid Depicts Perils of Unsafe Sex." *Billboard* 4 Apr. 1995: 53.

Sandler, Adam. "Hollywood Shines Light on Pop Icons." *America*

Online. AOL News Profiles. 19 July 1996.

Saxberg, Lynn. "Melissa: Her Latest Album's Become an Anthem for Some Young Women." *Ottawa Citizen* 28 May 1992.

Schoemer, Karen. "Fast Car." *Spin* 1989: 76, 78–79.

Schwartz, Deb. "Love and Marriage." *Out* June 1996: 88–98.

Segell, Michael. "A Fiery First." *Cosmopolitan* Mar. 1989: 52.

Selvin, Joel. "Etheridge Tries Out as Joplin: Singer Does Surprise Gig with Big Brother for Possible Janis Film." *San Francisco Chronicle* 4 June 1996: E1.

"She's the Only One." *Advocate* 30 May 1995: 71.

Shively, Debe. E-mail to the author. 18 Mar. 1996.

——. E-mail to the author. 4 May 1996.

Smith, C.M. "Melissa Etheridge's Rude Awakening." *Guitar Player* Oct. 1992: 18–19.

Soldan, Dawn. Telephone interview. 1 May 1996.

"Staying Close to the Stage: Melissa Etheridge Says Despite Experimentation, Her Focus Is on Live Music." *Akron Beacon Journal* 1994. *Newsbank*. Online. 2 Dec. 1996.

Stoliar, Joyce. E-mail to the author. 29 Sept. 1996.

Swenson, John. "Janis Joplin, Frank Zappa Reach Rock Hall of Fame." *Reuters News Service Online*. Online posting. 17 Mar. 1996.

"Talent in Action." *Billboard* 29 Oct. 1988: 28.

Tomlinson, Stuart. "Etheridge on Her Brand of Blues: 'I Believe It Comes from the Soul.' " *Oregonian* 24 Feb. 1989.

Tough, Paul. "The Time of Their Lives." *Savvy Woman* July 1989: 18–20.

Trakin, Roy. "Changes in Attitude." *Music Express* May 1992: 9, 10, 13.

Troila, Judy. Interview. *Melissa Etheridge Information Network Newsletter* 1.1.

Vare, Ethlle Ann. "Melissa Etheridge." *Hollywood Reporter* 3 Sept. 1992: 9, 17.

Wagley, Rayna. Telephone interview. 16 Mar. 1996.

Walters, Barry. "A Rock Goddess Comes Out." *Advocate* Apr. 1993: 77.

"What I Watch." *TV Guide* 6 May 1995: 5.

Whitall, Susan. "Melissa Etheridge Joins Rock's New Songwriting Sisterhood." *Detroit News* 24 Mar. 1989: D1.

Willman, Chris. "Ace of Abasement." *Entertainment Weekly* 17 Nov. 1995: 76–77.

Wurtzel, Elizabeth. "Backyard Party." *New York* 13 Nov. 1989: 114 18.

Wyatt, Hugh. "Rhythm on the Rebound." *New York Daily News* 28 May 1988.

Zaslow, Jeffrey. "Melissa Etheridge: 'Show Who You Are.'" USA *Weekend* 27–29 Jan. 1995: 30.

Zollo, Paul. "Melissa Etheridge's Little Secret." *Musician* Jan. 1996: 22–35.